Dr. King, The Rabbi, and Me:
A Connecticut Journey

Carol-Anne Hossler

HAND IN HAND PRESS LLC

Dr. King, The Rabbi, And Me: A Connecticut Journey
Published by Hand in Hand Press LLC
3816 East Saint Remy Drive
Bloomington, Indiana 47401
www.drkingandme.com

Copyright 2020 by Hand in Hand Press LLC

ISBN 978-1-7340831-0-1
ISBN 978-1-7340831-1-8 (pbk.)
ISBN 978-1-7340831-2-5 (ebook)

Requests for information should be directed to the author at the publisher's mailing address

All rights reserved. No part of this book may be reproduced or transmitted in any form or by any means, electronic or mechanical, including photocopying and recording, or by any information storage and retrieval system, with permission in writing from the publisher.

Cover design by Gregg Litchfield
Author photography on back cover by Rodney Margison

*To David and Peter and all teachers, who,
like Rabbi Rubenstein care, listen and lead the way.*

Acknowledgments

This book is the result of years of storytelling and could not have been written without the help of several people especially Rabbi Byron Rubenstein who invited me to hear and meet Dr. Martin Luther King Jr. The Rabbi's legacy is described as "kindness, teaching and civil rights justice." Those life qualities worked well for me because without his invitation and willingness to set up the meeting I had with Dr. King, there would be no story.

My thanks to those who helped as I researched. Mrs. Suzanne Rubenstein shared valuable information about that memorable evening. Temple Israel administrative staff provided guidance: Sandy Silverstein, Lisa Goldberg, and Debra Pinals. Cynthia P. Lewis, Director of Archives, at the King Library in Atlanta, Georgia, located the program for the May 22, 1964, Rededication Service at Temple Israel. Amy Jackson and Lesley Levin helped me better understand the religious service that I attended. Jane Smith, Holiday House counselor, made several significant contributions to this story.

Several people assisted me with this daunting process. My thanks to them. Janet Cheatham Bell and Heidi Newman served as editors. Jesus Garcia played a pivotal role in shaping this book. Lynne Boyle-Baise, Zac Casey, Kathryn Engebretson, and Pat Wilson read the manuscript and made important content suggestions. Erna Alant, Keith Barton and Carolyn Emmert inspired me to continue on. Trisha Ulrich provided an upper elementary classroom teacher critical eye. Merridee LaMantia and Gregg Litchfield had a vision of what the book could look like; Rodney Margison assisted with the many technicalities of final book production; Linda Margison shepherded the manuscript to final book format.

I am indebted to my parents, Barbara and Bob Hughes. They made important choices about the church we attended and welcomed girls from New York City into our home. Those decisions set the stage for my meeting with Martin Luther King Jr.

Finally, it is with love and deep appreciation that I acknowledge my husband, Don Hossler. His encouragement and support made me believe that this dream could become a reality.

Author's Note

I have shared this story to students of all ages in schools, churches, and Boys & Girls Clubs. It is a story about civil rights unrest, President Kennedy's assassination and teenage traumas; those events triggered my conversation with Dr. Martin Luther King Jr.

As a teenager in 1963, I thought about freedom and equality and began to understand that my life was easier – much easier – than lives lived by kids who were not white. I know now that some white, middle class kids at that time, paid attention to the Civil Rights Movement and saw the different realities, some did not. I was removed from the heat and heart of the civil rights movement, but I was curious about it, wanted to learn more and be part of it because I understood about "what's fair." Like all Americans, I witnessed an important time in our country's history.

The use of the word Negro in this book is historically correct and is used in the diary portions of the text. Since language and vocabulary changes over time, I intentionally used black in the postscript portions of the text. The "Breaking News" portions of the book are headlines that I have created and in several instances are exaggerated in order to make a point.

That evening experience had a huge impact on me and in fact, has encouraged me over time. I always wished that this story could have a wider audience. I hope that Rabbi Rubenstein's generosity towards me and Dr. King's message will also inspire you.

Carol-Anne Hossler
Bloomington, Indiana

Table of Contents

Merry Lane 11

Hanging Around 45

Connecticut Crossings.. 71

Humdrum and The March on Washington...................... 77

Interruptions and Special Announcements.................... 87

New Possibilities and Ideas... 103

Sleepover and Sadness 117

Dance Parties 139

Here and There News... 161

February Ups and Downs 171

Considerations: Shoplifters and MLK............................. 183

The Telephone Call... 193

The Meeting... 205

Merry Lane
April 1963

Tuesday, April 9

When I was 12, I couldn't wait to become a teenager. I thought I'd feel differently when I turned 13 on March 30, but it's not working out like that at all. We still live in the same house on Merry Lane. My family is just the same as before – Mom, Dad, Nana, and us three girls. We moved here two years ago but I still feel new. It takes forever to make new best friends.

I always say Judy is my best friend, but she lives 70 miles away in West Hartford, Connecticut. We've only met once, when her family came to visit. Our dads are best friends, but I didn't get that figured out until last summer when I heard Mom and Dad talking about getting together with the Bramleys. I had no idea why I needed to meet these people. I was angry because since they were coming, I couldn't have dinner at a new friend's house and that was the first time I had been invited over. My parents tried to get me excited about the visit by saying, "They have a daughter your age, Carol-Anne."

I didn't care.

Judy's family came for dinner. The dads were all goofy and acted like the 13-year-old boys I know at school. Mom called from the kitchen to ask Dad to put another chair at the table. So, he and Uncle Don carried our biggest stuffed upholstered chair from the living room into the dining room. The dads and daughters were laughing, but when the moms saw the chair, they weren't.

Here's Judy!

When Judy and I went up to my room to talk, we found we had a lot in common. She's got one older brother and I have two little sisters, but school, teachers and kids are the same. Since that visit, we've been pen pals.

Judy's great, but what I want is someone my age right here in Weston, someone to talk to and go to school with, and maybe to Girl Scouts. Someone besides my sister, Nancy, who is 9 and always has her nose in a book.

Judy's birthday is tomorrow, and she'll be 13, too. I still have to get her a gift and have Mom mail it. Judy is always on time and writes back immediately. Not me. It takes me forever to get anything in the mail to her. She got me this diary, and I know she keeps one and probably writes every day. I'm promising myself to write in this one 'til it's full. Nana says I'll be glad if I do because it's like writing to your future self and maybe even your kids. That's weird to think about.

The only diary I've read is *The Diary of Anne Frank* and my life isn't anything like Anne's. There's no war going on. She lived in a big city and was squished in that attic with her family and those other people and couldn't go out for fear of her life. I live out in the country. It takes 10 minutes to walk to the next house, or to walk home from the school bus stop. There are woods, hills and old stone fences everywhere. Our house is roomy, and it's very safe. My diary will be dull, compared to Anne Frank's. I'll have to do more thinking so it isn't too boring.

My dad tells me I'm too "young to know what I think." I can't tell if he is joking. I bet Anne Frank's dad didn't tell her that.

I want to get *Judy Cherry Ames, Staff Nurse* for her birthday. I loved it, even though it reminded me of my favorite, *Cherry Ames, Dude Ranch Nurse*. Hopefully tomorrow we can go to the bookstore so I can get Judy's present in the mail before she turns 14.

Wednesday, April 10

Yesterday when I went downstairs to remind Mom about Judy's birthday present, she told me to watch Linda since Nana was busy hemming Nancy's Easter dress. I amused Linda for a half hour until Mom and Dad got back from the Cannondale train station. Nancy had to set the table since I was busy with the baby.

Our family still calls Linda "the baby" but I think we should stop. She's 2 ½, has a mouthful of teeth, talks up a storm and sometimes is very bossy. That's not a baby. Besides, "Linda" is a perfectly good name. So is "Nancy." How come I got a double name, hyphenated? What were my parents thinking? At home, it's always "Carol-Anne" but at school, teachers and kids always call me "Carol," which is just a shortcut so that they don't really have to say my real, longer name. Nana calls me "Carolee" and I like it, but I wouldn't want anyone else calling me that.

Today Mom took Linda to pick up Dad at the train station. Nana's downstairs waiting so we can get the card game going and watch Walter Cronkite and the *CBS Evening News*.

I bet we hear more about the boycotts and the sit-ins at the lunch counters in Birmingham, Alabama. That gloomy stuff is always on the news.

Above are my sisters, Nancy on the left and Linda on the right.

Thursday, April 11

At choir practice today, I tried out for the Mother's Day anthem solo and got picked. I want to keep this a secret from Mom. I told Nancy not to say anything.

We always stop at the drugstore in Weston after school on Thursdays to get ice cream and so Mom can buy her cigarettes. Then we drive to church in Wilton for choir practice. Mom says the ice cream cones "tide us over." After choir practice, we bought new dress shoes for Easter. Finally! Slip-ons with a little heel! Nancy got Mary Janes. Mom bought cards for me to write the much dreaded birthday thank-you notes. I'm supposed to be writing to my great aunts for the clothes they sent, but I don't have to write to Mom's sister, Aunt Bette. She invited me to New York City to see the musical *Oliver!* Mom said it's all right if I don't write a thank-you until after the trip. I like the yellow material Mom got me for a new spring coat. She also said "saying" thank you was enough for her and Dad. Gee, thanks, Mom.

Friday, April 12

School was the usual this week – homeroom, English, math, social studies, PE, French, science, and Home Ec. And then there is the little secret world at the back of social studies class. Does our teacher Mr. Butler even know?

I sit in the back of the classroom, and up-front Mr. Butler talks on and on. I don't even know what he's talking about... nothing I'm really interested in. At the same time, Rita Walsh is dishing out fireball candies to Billy Beboe and other kids. Usually she charges a nickel. When she feels generous, she gives me one, but not too often. I don't bring money to school, so I can't buy them from her. I don't understand how Mr. Butler doesn't realize what's going on. The kids with fireballs end up having red lips and smelling of cinnamon.

Saturday, April 13

Tomorrow's Easter, so we boiled and decorated eggs. Mom and I will hide them for Nancy and Linda tonight.

On the front page of our *New York Times* today, there was a story about Dr. Martin Luther King Jr. When we talk about "current events at school" it's usually something about the Soviet Union Luna launch missing the moon, or the Academy Awards, or Winston Churchill becoming an honorary US citizen, or the Mets. We don't usually talk about what's going on with the civil rights movement.

Our minister, Mr. Greene, is always talking about the civil rights movement and how Negro people ought to be treated fairly in our country. Dr. King is in jail. He got arrested yesterday in Birmingham, Alabama. He was probably protesting or marching through the streets again. They said he was parading without a permit or license or something. Some people said it was "demonstrating." I think people should talk out disagreements before they start demonstrating. Demonstrations can be dangerous because people get hurt. I'm really glad they don't happen around here. I wonder what Mr. Greene will say about Dr. King's arrest. Mrs. King just had a baby and with Dr. King in the spotlight and not at home, that must be tough on their family.

Who would want to be in solitary confinement? Credit: Adam Jones, Ph.D./Global Photo Archive/Wikimedia Commons

Sunday, April 14

When we got up this morning, the "Easter Bunny" had shown up and left baskets with chocolate candy and that plastic grass that grows on its own. Best of all, there's the marshmallow Peeps. I ate all of mine before we piled into the car for the drive to Wilton.

Church took forever. All the people who don't usually come suddenly show up. The best part of the service was the singing. There were two worst parts: the smell of the Easter lilies and the long sermon. Since I am in the choir, we sit up front, and those lilies smelled like a perfume factory. The choir kids see Mr. Greene from behind, with his robe and bald head. He always moves around a lot, but today he moved around more than usual. Once again in his sermon, he mentioned Martin Luther King Jr. being in the Birmingham jail. Dr. King is in solitary confinement and hasn't talked with his wife or anybody, so people are nervous about that. He and some other people were protesting because of the segregation in Birmingham. Dr. King's best friend, Ralph Abernathy, is in the same jail but I guess they can't be in solitary confinement together. If I was in jail, I'd like to share a cell with my best friend. I wonder what Judy would think about that. I suppose it would depend on the reason for being locked up.

When we finally got home, the phone was ringing. It was Ahmee and Grandpa Ray calling from California to say, "Happy Easter." When they call, I only get to say a quick "hi" because it's so expensive. Anyway, my grandparents called because they are leaving soon on a trip around the world. No more monthly calls for a while. Their last stop will be Merry Lane for a family Thanksgiving. It seems so far off. Ahmee said she would send postcards and bring presents from the places they visit.

Enough for today. Nancy and Linda's Peeps haven't been eaten yet so now I must convince them to share with me.

Monday, April 15

I love Mondays because *Time* magazine is always here waiting when I get home from school. When we lived in New Jersey, Mom and Dad saved all the *Time* magazine covers to use as wallpaper in our basement family room. When *Time* came, Mom removed the cover right away and pasted it up. I didn't read magazines then, but I liked to look at those covers.

Today in *Time* I read about two new movies: *The Birds* and *To Kill a Mockingbird*. *The Birds* sounds creepy. *To Kill a Mockingbird* is supposed to be good but scary in a different way. Even though our family never goes to the movies, I do like reading about them. I'll read *To Kill a Mockingbird* this summer. Judy keeps asking me if I have. Not yet, Judy.

Tuesday, April 16

Spring is coming to Connecticut. I always like it when the woods green up. When we lived in Pennsylvania, it was the country but not like Merry Lane. Connecticut is covered with over 60,000 miles of old stone wall fences that zigzag all over the place. Who on earth bothered to measure them? I don't like going too close because copperhead snakes live around them. One thing we don't have on Merry Lane is next-door neighbors because our street is long and there are only five houses on it.

Wednesday, April 17

I got a ten-page letter from Judy today. Blab. Blab. Blab. How does she sit and write for that long? It will take me forever to write something long enough to send back to her. What will I write about?

Judy must grill her father about his boyhood stories. He tells her about the friendship he had with my dad and the friendship our grandparents had in the 1930's; her letters include all the details. Today she wrote that our grandparents played cards together during the depression. (What's that mean? I thought "depression" was a bad mood.) She said one time our dads put a toilet on top of a neighbor's house. That adventure made the local newspaper, and they both got in big trouble.

I can't imagine my father doing anything like that. These

days he gets up, eats breakfast and then Mom drives him three miles to catch the 7:11 train from the Cannondale station to New York City. At the end of the day, she picks him up and brings him home for our 7:15 family dinner. No silliness.

Judy writes to me and I write back but not as quickly. I feel a little guilty about that. Her life is interesting. Her long letters are filled with details galore. She writes about her friends and what they do together. I think I know Judy's friends Candy and Jillian just about as well as she does.

BREAKING NEWS
King STILL Locked Up!

Thursday, April 18

At choir today, Miss Sallinger had me sing my solo. I still don't know all the words.

It was a rush tonight because I had lots of math homework. It doesn't matter if it's just the odd or just the even problems, it takes me *forever* because math is hard for me. My teacher, Mrs. Herbert tells me: "Work through the struggle, you're going to be fine. You can learn this!" I'm glad she thinks so.

I like reading and I've made a discovery about myself: I like telling stories. In English class, I learned how to stretch out the writing so it will be as long as it needs to be. Talk about character development and sprinkle in quotes from the text with a few quotation marks. Those tactics always take care of the page number issue. I should try that when I write to Judy.

Martin Luther King Jr. is still locked up and in the news

because of a letter he is writing from jail. People say he is writing it on toilet paper and in the margins of newspaper articles. The letter has been smuggled out by friends who visit. The whole thing is incredible: minister in jail because he didn't have the right papers for walking down the road, a secret letter written and broadcast on national television and published in some newspapers. It's like watching a movie that is never over. I think the boys in social studies class would love talking about a secret letter written on toilet paper for current events even if it has something to do with civil rights stuff.

Saturday, April 20

It's Saturday, so that means GFS, which is one church activity I really love. GFS stands for Girls' Friendly Society. Our motto is "Bear ye one another's burdens," so we try to find ways to help others. We meet at 10:00 on Saturday mornings. All the other girls wear slacks but not Nancy and me. Mom and Dad say, "You are going to church, so you have to wear a skirt or a dress." It's ridiculous. It makes me and Nancy

Why does a silly pin mean so much to me?

really stand out, which we already do since we are the only girls from Weston. Even Miss Simpson, our GFS leader, wears slacks. She's older than us kids but probably younger than Mom and Dad. Miss Simpson wears glasses like mine and I'm almost as tall as she is. I don't tell anyone about GFS because its name is so stupid. But actually, GFS girls really are friendly and nice. I wish the girls at school were.

At GFS we have a short worship service, work on service projects and talk a lot. Miss Simpson lets us plan the meetings, but she always has something for us to talk about, usually some important news issue. That's the best part of the club for me. Today Miss Simpson asked if we knew the difference between segregation and integration. The older girls knew segregation meant keeping the Negro people separate from white people and integration meant bringing everyone together.

Vickie said, "Desegregation and integration mean the same thing." I'm glad she mentioned it because I didn't know that for sure.

Miss Simpson commented, "Do you remember Mr. Greene's sermon last week? He was talking about the civil rights movement, and especially everything going on in Birmingham." Of course, everyone – well, at least us older girls – answered "Yes," even though we might not remember *everything*. Then Miss Simpson asked, "Is patience *always* a virtue?" I think she asked because Dr. King's letter replied to white church leaders who were asking Negro people to slow down and be patient about civil rights. Dr. King said that his people had waited long enough. He said people had a duty to disobey unjust laws. Really? It's OK to disobey a bad law? I'm not sure about that. But then, what if the unfair law NEVER changes?

Miss Simpson asked what we thought about that. We talked about white kids and Negro kids getting along with each other. There aren't any Negro kids in our area, so we aren't very integrated even though there aren't any laws saying we must be segregated.

Sunday, April 21

Yesterday at GFS, we talked about civil rights. Today, we listened to it again during the sermon. Our minister went on and on about civil rights and the South. After church at the coffee hour, small groups of adults stood around and talked.

Mr. Greene talked about something St. Augustine said about "an unjust law being no law at all." I think Dr. King talked about St. Augustine, too. I don't know anything about St. Augustine, but what he said about unjust laws makes sense to me. If it is law in our country, I guess – no – I think it better be fair for everybody. Some church people agreed with Mr. Greene but not everyone. One lady told Mom that he shouldn't have talked about civil rights on Easter Sunday.

I have to memorize the words for my Mother's Day solo so during the sermon I wrote the words out on the church bulletin for practice:

God be in my head and in my understanding. God be in my eyes and in my looking. God be in my mouth and in my speaking. God be in my heart and in my thinking. God be at my end and at my departing.

I like it except for thinking with my heart. That should be the "head" part. And I don't like thinking about "my departing" which sounds like I'm almost dead. Mom will cry when I sing, which will mean she liked it.

Monday, April 22

Today a doctor in Houston, Texas, put an artificial heart into a man. I hope nobody in my family ever needs a new heart. If a man gets a new heart, does it mean he will start *thinking* differently?

Title of the next Cherry Ames book? *Cherry Ames, Artificial Heart Surgical Nurse.*

Wednesday, April 24

Mom's gone to the station and I am sitting on the loveseat in Nana's room. She's watching the news but I'm going to write about school. Hopefully I can get this entry finished before dinner.

Every morning I walk to the bus stop with Nancy, but I try not to sit by her on the bus. I like to sit behind this girl with an amazing beehive hairdo. How does she get her hair to stand that high? She must use a can of hairspray every morning. The bus stops at Nancy's school first; my school is brand new and a little farther out. Of all the schools I've been to in New Jersey, California, Pennsylvania and Connecticut, this is the nicest building, but the kids seem the least friendly. Every time we've moved, Mom has always said, "Make new friends, keep the old. One is silver and the other, gold." But it doesn't really work that way. She wants me to think it's easy to move but it takes time to make a real friend.

At school, I put my stuff in my locker and go to Mrs. Gleason's homeroom. Mrs. Gleason sits at the front and doesn't talk to anyone. Some kids say she has a drinking problem and keeps a bottle of scotch in her desk drawer. Some kids say she is getting a divorce. She never smiles. If someone approaches her with a question, she raises her head, looks straight ahead and responds. She never looks at the kid. Her children go to school here, too. Sometimes they stop in, but she doesn't look at them or talk much to them, either.

I really love my math teacher, Mrs. Herbert and she has beautiful fingernails. She always thinks that I can learn math. She doesn't have a favorite student – a teacher's pet. So even though the class is hard for me, I don't mind going because Mrs. Herbert is always there, and she always helps. PE is next. In PE, we have awful gym uniforms, a pair of red shorts with the shirt attached – all one piece. We're playing field hockey right now.

English class is after lunch, and it can be fun because I like reading books and poetry. But the teacher is snobby and has teacher's pets. The teacher's pets get so stuck up. We have French every day. Class time is better than language lab time. Language lab is so tedious and just about puts everyone to sleep, listening to those same phrases over and over. *Comment allez-vous? Comment allez-vous?*

Mondays, Wednesdays, and Fridays we have social studies; Tuesdays and Thursdays we have science. Twice a week the girls have home economics with Mrs. Dangerfield. We cook. We sew. It's not much fun but we sit at tables instead of desks. Next year we'll switch with the boys for one week of shop.

I can't wait for Saturday and my birthday present from Aunt Bette – a trip to New York City!

Friday, April 26

We got a postcard from Ahmee and Grandpa Ray. They loved Hawaii with all the flowers, beautiful beaches, a luau and mangoes. Ahmee loves mangoes. Next stop is Japan.

I'm packed for New York City and I'll write again next week.

Monday, April 29

What a weekend! I was worried about going to New York City since I never have taken the train alone before. The train wasn't crowded, which was good because I didn't want to sit next to anyone. Dad drove me to the Westport train station. I took the first window seat I could find and waved to him. When we pulled out of the station, everything looked familiar. Then, country turned to city with tall buildings, sidewalks, overpasses, cars stopping and going and the sound of the DING-DING-DING-ding-ding as the train raced past the crossings. I saw the tenements and the fire escapes and thought of *West Side Story*. The buildings looked broken down and dirty. There was a lot of graffiti – colorful but gloomy and frightening since I didn't know what the letters and symbols meant. Looking out the window I realized how

Lady Liberty stands with the New York City skyline in the distance.

glad I am to live in the country and not the city. We have dirt but not like the city dirt.

Aunt Bette was waiting at the station, just as Mom said she would be. We went to a fancy restaurant with a buffet and so many food choices, it was unbelievable. I showed self-control until dessert, when I took two dishes of ice cream. After lunch, we went to the matinee of Oliver. It was the second Broadway show I've seen. Last year, Mom, Nancy, Aunt Bette and I went to *The Sound of Music*. After that performance, Nancy almost fell into the orchestra pit. She wanted to see the violins.

Seeing *Oliver!* made me want to sing. I can't wait to get the LP record so I can learn the words to all the songs. Charles Dickens wrote the story about a little orphan boy and his struggles growing up. Fortunately, it has a happy ending. I love happy endings. I'm going to read *Oliver Twist*.

After the play, even though we didn't see the Statue of Liberty, I bought a Miss Liberty postcard to send to Judy. Aunt Bette bought me a yellow pillbox hat that goes great with the yellow spring coat Mom made me. Jacqueline Kennedy wears pillbox hats. She looks great in them with her perfect hair.

On the way home Sunday, the train was much more crowded. I found a seat next to an older woman. As I sat down, she started to talk. She said she was going to visit her family and that she was lonely because she didn't see them very often. When she got off at her stop, I slid over to the window to watch her meet them. There they were, her son and three grandchildren. It didn't seem like they lived so far away that the lady should feel lonely. I wonder if Nana is lonely. I am going to ask her.

Tuesday, April 30

Three weeks of writing and it's more entertaining than I thought it would be. Usually I can't stay within the space for one day. I reread what I have written, and it seems like all I write about is me and what's going on in my life. It's all I know. At least I am writing several times a week. Somebody once told me "a promise is sacred." This must be true, even if you just promise yourself to write in a diary.

When Nana and I were playing Canasta tonight, I asked if she was lonely and she said, "No, Carolee, I am not." I felt happy for her and for us, too. It's wonderful living with your grandmother, especially when she spoils you as much as Nana spoils Nancy, Linda and me.

While Mom and Linda went to pick up Dad tonight, Nancy played cards with Nana and me. It seems like Nancy has all the luck because she always wins. She gets "good" cards and then she cheats by looking at the reflection in Nana's and my glasses. She's such a brat sometimes. We play cards in the kitchen so we can pay attention to dinner as it cooks, and Nana watches the news on the TV.

I don't like watching the news because it's like listening to a sermon in the middle of the week. All we see are pictures of Negro people from the South demonstrating and white people being awful. Even though I don't like watching, I'm kind of hooked because I can't believe how the white people act. Why are the white people – people who look like me – so mean? There's always someone getting killed because of the civil rights movement – white people, too. Last week a white man died because he was against segregation.

Postscript from Carol-Anne
2020

Do you know what a postscript is? Before email, texts and cell phones, people wrote letters or sent postcards. Telephone calls, especially long-distance calls, were very expensive. Most kids did not own phones.

A postscript – P.S. – was written at the end of the letter because the writer wanted to add more information. Sometimes it is just a sentence, sometimes, more. You might find a P.S. at the end of a chapter because as I reflect on my life in 1963, I realize that I've learned lessons and my thinking has changed. Some people might say that I have had a "change of heart." Lessons learned and some of my new ideas can be found in the postscripts.

May 1963

Wednesday, May 1

It's spring, so the walk home from the bus stop seems miles longer. When it's raining, Mom picks us up. Most of the time we walk by the two houses just off Route 57 and down the hill past woods, woods, woods. I realized today why the walk is always longer in the spring: deer flies.

Deer fly season in Connecticut means trouble because deer fly bites really hurt. Nancy is afraid of bugs, especially bees and deer flies. Today as we got off the bus, our neighbor, Mrs. Farrington, pulled up in her big fancy station wagon, picked up her two kids, and drove home. She didn't ask if we wanted a ride, even though there's room. She never asks. Nancy, Frances and I ran down the hill as fast as we could to stay ahead of the deer flies.

We never talk to the Farringtons. When we moved into our house, Mrs. Farrington called to tell us to stay inside when their brindle dog was outside because their dog bites. Nice. Mrs. Farrington is our neighbor, but we don't like her because she is such a sourpuss. She never waves or smiles when she drives by. Our family calls her "Mrs. Oots." It suits her better because that nickname sounds disagreeable.

We like our neighbors the Lindseys. They just moved from England. Frances is a year younger than me and has a strong accent, so sometimes she's hard to understand. I like her but not as a best friend. She lives with her mom, dad, brother and auntie. One February afternoon, I was at Frances' and I was invited to "tea." They don't just have tea. They have cookies, tea sandwiches and tasty candies. Mrs. Lindsey served tea in fancy teacups at the dining room table. Auntie passed around all the treats. Wow! Why don't we have teatime in the United States?

Another interesting thing about teatime was the talking. Frances, Mrs. Lindsey and Auntie talked about life in England, the fun, and everything they miss. I talked about our life in New Jersey, California and Pennsylvania, places we used to live. They are lonely for England and want to go "home." Every time I've moved, I wished to be back at the other place – the place that was home. I hope they don't move because then I wouldn't have anyone to talk to after school. It's nice having Frances around.

BREAKING NEWS
Negro Kids Ditch School
and Are ARRESTED!

Thursday, May 2

We stopped playing cards tonight and watched the news instead. Walter Cronkite must have been sick because Harry Reasoner took his place. Harry Reasoner's daughter is in my class at school. She's very quiet.

A lot went on today in Birmingham. Negro kids ditched school to protest not being able to shop freely – wherever they want – in downtown Birmingham stores. Instead of going to school, they went to the Sixteenth Street Baptist Church, headquarters for the civil rights movement. They spent the morning singing hymns and civil rights songs and praying. I can't imagine walking out of school unless Mom was picking me up or I was headed home on the school bus.

At 1:00, kids in groups of fifty at a time left the church singing "We Shall Overcome." Some carried "Freedom Now" signs. Parents and supporters encouraged them from a park across the street. Outside the church the kids were met by the police. That's when they knelt down to pray. The Director of Public Safety, Bull Connor, had the kids arrested. School buses took them – not home – but to jail. Harry Reasoner said 900 kids got picked up. That's more than everyone in my entire school. Even though the kids were hauled off, they looked happy.

I have never heard of children being arrested. How can they do that? Does Bull Connor think he makes the laws in Birmingham? Doesn't he have to pay attention to the laws of our country? What are they going to do with kids in jail? What about dinner, bath time and homework? Pictures on the news show the police hitting kids. I thought the police were there to help and take care of people not hurt them. I guess sometimes they protect people but not always. What a mess. Deer flies don't seem so bad. Not as bad as all the trouble in Birmingham.

And why would parents name a kid "Bull?"

Friday, May 3

Newscasters are calling yesterday's event in Birmingham the "Children's Crusade." The students who protested are in jail. More kids didn't go to school today and their parents are encouraging them. It seems like most people think that what the kids are doing is right. I wouldn't want to skip school because I think that would lead to trouble for me but the reasons for the Children's Crusade seem fair and sensible. A store should sell to anyone with money, shouldn't it, no matter what their skin color?

It was different today because Bull Connor had a new plan which could be called "Clubs and Dogs." Police officers carried billy clubs and had German Shepherd dogs on leashes. The dogs were barking, jumping up and attacking kids. Firemen sprayed water on kids. The water was strong, and I bet it really hurt. One newscaster said the "force of the water could tear bark from an oak tree." Those poor kids quickly turned so the water whacked them on their backs. One kid was thrown off his feet and lifted into the air. He landed on the pavement and slip-slid down the sidewalk. There was a lot of screaming. Over 2,000 kids are in jail now – some as young as 5 years old! Thank goodness I don't live there and I'm not a Negro.

I can't get the pictures of the German Shepherds, the water hoses and the kid slamming down onto wet pavement out of my mind. It was frightening. All this nastiness just because some Americans want to be treated fairly. What happened to "the land of the free and the home of the brave"? Doesn't that mean everybody? If I hadn't seen the TV news clips, I'd think it was somebody's creative writing assignment. It's awful to think about!

So now, I'll change the subject. At dance class tonight I get to wear a dress mom didn't make for me and it's the last class of the year. Thank goodness. I don't like going to ballroom dance class because I'm so tall, the boys are so short, I'm always last to be chosen, and I usually get stuck with Billy Beboe. He is about two feet shorter than me, and from the look on his face I can tell that he wishes he wasn't at ballroom dance class, too.

Sunday, May 5

Today was a normal Sunday for the Hughes family. That means that this morning was a "rat race" because it's always a mess getting five people ready for 9:00 church. There's lots of confusion and when we finally all end up in the car, it takes a few minutes for everyone to calm down. After church and Sunday school, the Sunday morning routine finishes up with coffee cake and quiet time. My parents read the paper in the living room. I read about the Children's Crusade; the article said that the Birmingham police arrested ten kids per minute.

The sermon today was about the Children's Crusade. I sat in the choir loft and listened to every word Mr. Greene said. The other kids were listening, too. Mr. Greene kept asking what the teachings of the church tell us to do. How are we supposed to act? Is this what God wants from us? I don't think so. For me, the Birmingham news stories seem so far away. I watch and I listen. Then I get to turn the TV off if it gets too bad for me.

Monday, May 6

I love reading *Time* magazine, especially the stories about princesses and queens. Today in the "People" section, there was a story about Princess Grace of Monaco. She used to be a movie star. She's from Philadelphia, so we might have been neighbors. (*Ha!*) Probably every girl dreams of being a princess when she grows up. Princess Grace's dream came true.

The Children's Crusade went on again today. Dr. King said about 2,500 people – he meant kids – were in the Birmingham jail. People from all over are going to Birmingham to encourage and support them. I bet next week there will be tons of information in *Time*. Everyone hopes that this crusade will be over soon.

I wonder if the Negro girls who sit in jail ever dream of

being princesses. Right now, I bet they are just dreaming about going home.

Wednesday May 8

Yesterday, I went with Frances to her horseback riding lesson. She wears special riding clothes with poufy pants (her jodhpurs). When we got to the stables, I saw the horse she was going to ride and then Mrs. Lindsey and I watched from the fence. I love watching Frances and her horse do the jumps.

Choir practice is tomorrow, and I know all the words for my solo by heart. Now, I just have to not be nervous when the 12th of May finally comes. I hope Nancy doesn't ruin the secret and tell Mom. After all, it is my Mother's Day present. Nana knows and is coming to church with us on Sunday.

While Mom and Linda went to the station, Nana, Nancy and I played gin rummy and watched the news, even though it's hard to look at. So much is happening because those kids walked out of school. People are mad at the police and firemen. The TV stations keep showing the pictures of the dogs, the fire hoses and the kids running and screaming. It's terrible. I've been thinking about the song "We Shall Overcome." We've sung that song in GFS, and on the bus coming home from school and I don't have to overcome anything, but I do love the tune and that song.

We shall overcome, we shall overcome. We shall overcome some day. Oh, deep in my heart, I do believe. We shall overcome someday.

While Negroes sing "We Shall Overcome" on TV, white people are yelling "Two, four, six, eight, we don't want to integrate."

Thursday, May 9

I didn't make any mistakes when I sang my solo at choir

practice today. I hope I can remember on Sunday. Miss Salinger told me to look at her, sing and pretend nobody else is around. I'll try, but it doesn't seem possible.

Friday, May 10

The Children's Crusade is over so that's good news. Desegregation will phase in little by little which means that Negroes still must be patient. In time, lunch counters, restrooms, fitting rooms and drinking fountains will not be labeled "Whites Only" or "Colored." Negro kids and their parents can shop where they want. It's also not going to cost *lots* of money to get kids out of jail. Good news! Does this mean that "all's right with the world" in Birmingham and everywhere else in the south now? I hope so but I'm not sure it will work out that way. It seems like such a struggle there. It isn't a problem in the North.

Today is my cousin Debbie's birthday. She is 13, too, like me. I wonder what she got for her birthday. She probably got some new fish for her aquarium. The last time we visited, Debbie told me that some of her fish eat their fish babies. *Sickening.*

Saturday, May 11

At GFS today, we decorated the Parish Hall for the Mother's Day coffee hour. Everyone was excited to arrange flowers in vases and put them on the tables with fancy tablecloths. It looked good when we finished.

At snack time, Miss Simpson asked us about the Children's Crusade. We talked about the kids being our ages. I said I didn't understand why Southerners would be so angry when all this has to do with is what's fair and what's not fair.

No surprise, Dr. King was right in the middle of the Children's Crusade turmoil. If I was his wife or child, I'd want him to stay home and take it easy. If the Birmingham police would arrest children, of course they'd arrest Dr. King. Even so, I can't figure out why the police would arrest a minister who preaches nonviolence.

And another "no surprise." The Gaston Motel where King and his friend were staying got bombed. I saw the pictures and I can't believe they weren't killed.

This civil rights stuff is much more interesting to me than studying about dates and dead people in social studies class at school.

Sunday, May 12

My Mother's Day solo was a huge success! Mom cried. Dad smiled. After church Nana hugged me and said, "Oh, Carolee! You did wonderfully!" I got so nervous as I sat in the choir loft and waited to sing. Just before my solo I needed to go to the bathroom. When it was time, the children's choir stood up and sang together. Then I sang by myself and finally, we all sang together one last time. At coffee hour, some of my parents' friends told me they liked my solo, too. I just sang and looked at Miss Salinger and that calmed my "butterflies" (that's what she called my nervousness). I'm glad it is over.

Monday, May 13

I didn't just read the "People," "Milestones," and "Cinema" sections of *Time* magazine today. I read "Dogs, Kids and Clubs." It said that some of the kids who walked out of school were younger than Nancy – just 5 years old. That nasty Bull Connor said, "Look at them run! I want to see the dogs work. Look at those n-----s run."

In the section called "We Shall Overcome," Dr. King told parents of the jailed children that the whole world was watching Birmingham. He thought since the whole world was watching, children would be safe. I don't know about that because the newspapers always write about what the segregationists say and do. It's safe where I live but I wouldn't feel safe if I lived in Birmingham and I was one of those kids.

Robert Kennedy, the President's brother, didn't think the children should participate. Not many white people did, but the kids sure got everyone's attention. If I did live in Birmingham and I was a Negro, I'm positive my parents wouldn't have let me walk out of school. And honestly, I don't think I would want to because I would be too afraid.

Wednesday, May 15

Today was Girl Scouts. I really liked being a Brownie but now I feel like quitting Girl Scouts. It seems babyish. There are only two other girls my age in the troop: Deirdre and Ellen. Ellen's mom, Mrs. Conley, is our troop leader. She is nice and lets us older Scouts do some responsibility-type things with the younger kids. Once I earn First Class, I'll quit and try something else. I just need four more badges until I'm a First Class scout.

At school today, Brooke Cornwell invited me to a sleepover this Friday with another girl, Winnie Bryant! I am excited because this is the first sleepover I have been to since we moved to Connecticut. I've heard about other sleepovers, but I wasn't invited. I'm glad Mom said I can go.

Saturday, May 18

What a sleepover! Mom picked me up two hours ago. I came home, ate a peanut butter and pickle sandwich and took a nap. Now to write about the amazing sleepover.

I took my things with me to school, and Winnie and I rode the bus home with Brooke. When we got there, she showed us her house and her bedroom. *Wow!* Brooke lives in a huge house, and she has a *cook* and a *butler*! It was like invited into a storybook. There were three beds in her bedroom, so it was perfect for a sleepover with two other girls. All three beds had beautiful matching yellow floral sheets, pillowcases and bedspreads. Our sheets don't all match. We had a snack and went up to Brooke's room to talk. Later, Brooke's mom called us downstairs because she wanted to meet Winnie and me. We said hello and then hurried back upstairs.

The cook called us to dinner. The three of us ate in the big dining room but not at the gigantic dining table, which had a crystal chandelier above it. We sat at a smaller table and even though it wasn't dark, we dined by candlelight. I loved looking out the window onto the beautiful front yard where I could see bright pink peonies almost ready to pop from bud into blossom. Brooke's parents didn't eat with us. We got served by the butler, James, who made sure we had everything we needed. He and Mary, the cook, were Negroes. After dinner, we watched TV – *Rawhide, The Addams Family* and *Gomer Pyle*. We talked and shared secrets and laughed until we couldn't stay awake any longer.

This morning, we ate breakfast in the kitchen. They had a curved booth just like the booths at coffee shops. Mary made us bacon, eggs and grits. I never had grits before and they tasted awful, like Cream of Wheat. At least I tried them, which is what Mom always tells me to do. After breakfast, we walked around Brooke's place. She showed us the tennis courts, the gardens, the pool and the horses in the barn. I felt like I was on a field trip. I hope I get invited back in the summer. I didn't meet Brooke's dad, and I just saw her mom for a minute. It was like Brooke was in charge.

Sunday, May 19

Today at church, no surprise, Mr. Greene talked about civil rights stuff and what's going on between whites and Negroes in the South. Civil rights. Civil rights. Civil rights. There's no getting away from it. We hear about civil rights daily on the radio and TV. It's all we see in the news. It's all we hear at church. Sometimes we talk about it at GFS. But even though we are studying American history we don't talk much about civil rights at school. Maybe it's because we don't have Negro kids at our school. If there were Negro kids in our class maybe they would bring the topic up.

    I don't know any Negroes. Brooke introduced me to Mary and James, but I don't really know them. Mary asked if I had any sisters or brothers. James was quiet but he wasn't scary. As we sat around the breakfast table, it was regular family table talk. Normal and nice. I wonder where Mary and James live. Weston is a small town, and I've never seen a Negro person in our town. Maybe they drive a distance to get to work.

    My parents tell me, and I hear at church, that there is no difference between white and Negro people that we are all the same. I have to say, though, there are some differences because we *look* different. It seems to me that being white must be easier; it must be harder to be a Negro person. When I was in fourth grade, we lived in Pennsylvania, and there was one Negro boy in my class. His name was George. After Thanksgiving everyone pulled a name out of a tin for a Christmas gift exchange. At the party, Mrs. Miller, our teacher, had a special way to exchange gifts. Each person opened his or her present in the front so everyone could see. Then the person had three guesses to discover who gave the gift.

    I got a beautiful pink scarf. Pink was my favorite color and I could tell all the girls thought my new scarf was beautiful. I made my three guesses and I was wrong, wrong, wrong! Then Mrs. Miller asked, "Who gave Carol this pretty scarf?" Slowly, George's hand went up. There was a pause and then everyone in the class laughed. But not me. I was so embarrassed. I really worked hard to hold back my tears.

I went home and told Mom what happened. From one moment to the next, that scarf went from beautiful to something to joke about. I was so ashamed. I really liked it, but everyone was laughing.

Mom told me that George's mom had called. She asked if it was okay for George to give me a scarf. My mom said, "Yes, that's fine," and then George's mom asked if I liked pink. My mother said, "Perfect, that's her favorite color." So, George's mom bought a special scarf just for me. I wore it to church, but I never wore it to school because I knew the kids would make fun of me and probably George, too. I felt bad for both of us.

Monday, May 20

This week, *Time* magazine is all about race problems and freedom. I try to skip reading about all the Birmingham nastiness, but I'm hypnotized by the stories and pictures. Plus, if I don't read it and Miss Simpson asks about the civil rights movement, I won't have anything to say and I get really embarrassed when that happens.

Tuesday, May 21

I got a long letter with tons of questions today from Judy. She even copied her favorite parts of the book she's reading. I prefer reading about her friends and the arguments they get into.

In June, Judy's coming to visit me for a week. In August, I'll visit her. It's going to be great. Judy wrote that we're going to the houses of two authors, Mark Twain and Harriet Beecher Stowe. Everyone knows who Mark Twain is, but I have no idea who the lady is. It's interesting that even though Judy and I don't live near each other, we can find so much to talk about. We use a lot of paper and share about books and authors that we like or don't like.

Wednesday, May 22

Tonight, Nana and I played cards, put the veggies on, amused Linda, and listened to the President's press conference. I wasn't *really* listening to President Kennedy tonight... until he started talking about corporal punishment. I asked Nana, "What's corporal punishment?" She said, "He's talking about spanking kids in school." Spanking kids in school? *Really?* President Kennedy is against it. Me, too.

Kids get taught "no hitting." Is spanking different from hitting? Obviously, some adults invented some ridiculous answer so that when they want to, they can hit kids just like the police did in Birmingham. If an adult hit me, I'd get angry and that wouldn't necessarily make me behave better.

Saturday, May 25

At GFS today the girls were talking about going to Holiday House. Since Nancy and I missed GFS last Saturday, we didn't know anything about it. Holiday House is the GFS summer camp. Most of the girls are going and it sounds fun. I brought a brochure home and asked my parents if I can go.

The brochure tells about Holiday House activities – swimming, canoeing, volleyball, and arts and crafts. Campers pay extra money for horseback riding, music and dance lessons. Since I have church choir and ballroom dance lessons at school, why would I pay extra money for that at camp? The outdoor chapel looks very...spiritual. It feels different when you pray outside, closer to God or something. Mom and Dad said they need to talk about it. What is there to talk about? Everybody is going and I want to go, too.

P.S. Since the sleepover, Brooke and Winnie haven't talked much to me.

Old Glory waves.

Monday, May 27

It's Memorial Day. I always get Labor Day and Memorial Day mixed up. I said that out loud, and Nana said, "Memorial Day starts with 'M' like May." That makes it easier.

Dad hung the flag up on the front porch. I like the way it looks, especially when it waves ever so slightly. Since there are only five families on our street, no one will notice. Frances's family is English and the people across the street are Irish; those neighbors probably don't care. When we hang the flag up it feels like we are being patriotic.

It's also Kentucky Derby Day. Everyone in our family bets on which horse will win. We put 25 cents into the pot and choose a horse. Nana gets excited and reads up on the horses. I chose On My Honor because that's the start of the Girl Scout pledge and as good a reason to choose a horse as any. My horse came in fourth. Nana's choice Chateaugay was the big winner. She won $1.25, probably enough for a big bag of M&M's, which she keeps in her top dresser drawer. It's her special stock, and she always shares.

Tuesday, May 28

In the "People" section of *Time* magazine this week there's another story about my favorite princess, Princess Grace of Monaco. She and her prince eat ham and eggs for breakfast. Their kids eat oatmeal. It's nice to know we have something in common. We eat oatmeal, too, but not in May. It's cold cereal season now.

Somebody in Princess Grace's family wanted to watch TV, so the hotel sent up five TV sets. Seems a bit much. Isn't it good for kids to learn to share?

Wednesday, May 29

Last Girl Scout meeting of the year. Two more badges to First Class.

Friday, May 31

I haven't written much about Linda, my littlest sister. It's easier to write about Nancy because she seems more like a real person. I probably make Nancy out to be worse than she really is. She loves to read, and she is quiet. Next year she is taking violin lessons. I am a little jealous, but she was the one who got chosen by the teachers, not me.

My littlest sister is very smart, just like Nancy. When she gets the giggles, we all giggle. She talks a lot and is kind of spoiled, but we like her that way. Linda is too cute to be annoying. Nancy must be past that stage. Nancy and I play a game that isn't really nice. When Linda is nearby, Nancy or I will say "Poof!" and then pretend that Linda has vanished. Then we go around saying, "Where's Linda?" Of course, she's standing right there, saying, "I'm here! I'm here!" but we just ignore her until Mom comes around and makes us stop. We aren't always mean, though. We read to her, sing with her and even play house with her dollies. Nancy plays with her a lot.

Tonight, Mom and Dad said I can go to Holiday House if I earn half of the cost, which turns out to be $38.50. It's a lot of money, but I can do it. Two weeks at camp! Hooray! I can't wait, but first I must earn the money.

Postscript from Carol-Anne
2020

When I think back to my 7th and 8th grade years I realize that sometimes in 1963 my thinking was incomplete and wrong. Now, I understand that some of my "wrong thinking" was what it was because I was only thinking about one point of view – my own. Where did I get my point of view? I think I got it from my parents, friends and other people I knew who had similar ideas.

In April and May of 1963, I thought about Dr. King scolding white people who wanted black people to be patient and wait for full citizenship and freedom. He said that it was OK to break some laws if they were "bad laws." That idea was new and confusing to me because I thought there weren't any "bad" laws; I was taught to obey rules, obey laws.

But in fact, I learned that some laws only worked well for certain people – white people. Those same laws were hurtful and unfair to other people – black people.

If I could go back to 1963 with a different point of view, a different opinion, it is possible that my thoughts, words and deeds would be kinder and fairer. I don't know for sure, but I like to think so.

What do you know about your own point of view? Has it ever changed?

Has there ever been a national news event that has been important to you? If so, what happened? Why is it important to you?

Hanging Around
June 1963

Sunday, June 2

I've got a plan for earning my Holiday House money. Mom and Dad will have some jobs around the house. I can babysit for my sisters and for the women's summer Bible study. Another girl, Janice, and I will watch kids in the church nursery. And I have Nana; she said she would help me and today she gave me $1.25. Since I already had $6.50, I have a decent start: $7.25 in my camp fund. I need to fill out camp registration papers tonight and turn them in on Saturday. Nancy doesn't want to go.

Two more weeks until summer vacation. Here's how my summer is planned:
- Now until June 23 – Earn money for Holiday House
- June 24 to June 28 – Judy's here
- June 29 to July 20 – Earn money for Holiday House
- July 4 – Breakfast, lunch, dinner and fireworks at Compo Beach
- July 21 to August 3 – GFS Camp at Holiday House
- August 12 to August 16 – My trip to visit Judy

Monday, June 3

Nothing about wearing glasses makes me feel pretty. I went to the eye doctor today and chose new glasses. Ugh. If I don't wear them, I can't see. If I do wear them, I feel ugly.

One thing though, my teeth are perfectly straight. Almost all the kids at school have braces on their teeth. When they get braces, they can hardly eat because the insides of their mouths are so sore. Although my teeth are straight and I brush daily, they are magnets for cavities. I dread going to the dentist because getting fillings really hurts. Our dentist has a huge window with birdfeeders to entertain patients when he drills. It doesn't distract me. The sound of the drill is nerve-wracking. I grab the arms of the chair and count the hairs in the dentist's nose. I don't understand why some kids get Novocain and I don't.

Not really my best look.

I wish I was shorter, had good vision and that Mom didn't sew all my clothes. My mom doesn't say so, but I guess it costs less for her to make our clothes instead of going to a department store to buy them. It's more fun to go shopping for clothes, not just fabric and a pattern.

Tuesday, June 4

Frances is the lucky one because she gets to have horseback riding lessons and today, I watched her again at her lesson. She's doing great. She's ready for competition. I bet she gets a ribbon.

My parents are going out on Saturday night. Nana is visiting her sisters in White Plains. That means I get to babysit Nancy and Linda and earn money for camp. Nancy doesn't like it when I say I am babysitting her, but when Nana is here, that is what we all call it, so why shouldn't I?

Got homework to do. Why do they give us homework when it's so close to the end of the school year?

Wednesday June 5

Today in English class instead of thinking about diagramming sentences, I thought about my sixth grade English teacher, Mr. Bowman. In his class, if you got 100% on all the spelling tests for the grading period, he'd make you a "Spelling Champion" plaque. The wooden plaques had your name inside a scroll-like thing with the words "6th Grade, Hurlbutt School, Weston, 1962." There was a little heart at the top. He'd hand out the plaques in class and say, "So and so deserves this award because he or she worked hard and did well on *all* the spelling tests this grading period." By the end of the year, five or six kids in our English class had earned them. Not me.

My spelling award – What a surprise!

I really wanted one of the Spelling Champion plaques, and I *did* study for the tests, but at least one time each grading period, I would mess up. It was very disappointing.

One summer Saturday morning, Mr. Bowman stopped by our house. He said he knew I worked to earn a Spelling Champion plaque. He made me a plaque because I'd been so close. My Spelling Champion plaque hangs over my desk and when I look at it, I remember Mr. Bowman. He didn't have to make that for me, but he did because he is one of the nicest teachers in the world.

Friday, June 7

One thing that's disgusting about our school is that there are girls who smoke in the bathroom. I don't know who they are, but they are always there, puffing away. Why doesn't the school do something about it? Bathrooms aren't the greatest places to be anyhow, but when those girls light up, the air just smells horrible. I try not to go in there – ever.

Mom smokes cigarettes and so do Nana and Aunt Bette. Dad smokes cigars or pipes sometimes after dinner. I don't like the smell of any smoke, yet I'm used to it at home, but it's worse at school.

Tomorrow night I am "taking care" of my sisters (that's what Mom said I have to say when Nancy is around) and I will be earning $$$. It's babysitting, if you ask me. *Yippee!*

Almost forgot! Sleepover at my house tonight with Brooke and Winnie. I can't wait. It is the first time I have had two girls invited over, and it should be loads of fun.

Saturday, June 8

The sleepover last night wasn't what I had hoped. Brooke and Winnie are such good friends. It wasn't like it was when we were at Brooke's house. And while we were together last night, Brooke let it slip that they had had a sleepover at Winnie's house. It sounded like a good time but guess what? I wasn't invited.

Sunday, June 9

Last night's babysitting was the worst. The worst.

Our house is out in the middle of nowhere. You can't see lights from any neighbor's home. Nancy, Linda and I ate dinner before Mom and Dad left. Mom said they would be home before 11:00. She left strict orders to put Linda to bed at 7:30.

Then Nancy and I could watch TV in the family room until they got home. We planned the TV schedule. Nancy chose *Flipper, Mr. Magoo* and *Gilligan's Island*. I chose *Saturday Night at the Movies*.

My parents left and I was babysitting! By 8:00, Linda was asleep, and Nancy and I were watching TV and munching on gingersnaps. Everything was fine until the doorbell rang at 10:30. We were scared out of our wits. Who would ring our doorbell at 10:30 at night? Nancy just looked at me. I had to do *something*. My heart raced as I tried to determine how to find out who was out there. So, I crawled – *no, I slithered* – into the front bathroom. I climbed up on the toilet and carefully lifted back the curtain above the high window, just enough to see who was out there.

Standing at the front door was a woman I didn't know. She had curlers in her hair and a scarf tied around her head. She held a cookie tin in her hands. She didn't look dangerous. Her car was parked in the driveway with the engine running and lights on. Thankfully, she never saw me. She rang the doorbell again. Then she turned, walked back to her car and drove away. Fifteen minutes later, Mom and Dad got home. I was so glad to see them. Nancy and I were still recovering from the scare. My parents had no idea who the lady was or why she was at our house.

Today at church, the mystery was solved. Mrs. Lilienthal told Mom that last night she stopped by to deliver cookies for the Canterbury Market, our church bazaar, which is coming up next weekend. She wanted to give them to Mom right away for the sweets booth. Why make cookies to donate a week before they will be sold? Mom and Dad said I did just the right thing by not answering the door. How could I? I was scared to death.

Camp count = $12.25

Monday, June 10

"Races: The Revolution" was an article in *Time* magazine today. It was upsetting to read because it talked about these past months a "time when the U.S. Negro's revolution for equality exploded on all fronts." I can believe it. All we see on TV, in magazines and in the newspaper are police dogs growling at Negroes, thousands of people going to jail, beatings, bombed homes and kids leading the parade. Something is always happening in the South. In Jackson, Mississippi, Negro protestors sat quietly at a five-and-ten lunch counter and tried to order lunch which doesn't seem like such a big deal. People are just trying to order lunch, right? But apparently, it is a big deal because then, white people poured ketchup, mustard and sugar all over the demonstrators who continued to utter not one word. So then, a former police officer hauled Negro Memphis Norman, 21, off his seat and beat him up. Norman was sent to the hospital and was charged with disturbing the peace. Really? Is sitting at a lunch counter "disturbing the peace?" Who really is misbehaving? Why isn't there someone there to stick up for people who are just trying to order lunch?

The word "revolution" keeps coming up. Some people say it's a "revolution for freedom," but that doesn't sound good to me. The word "revolution" sounds violent and it is hard to believe a "revolution" is happening in my own country.

I think the boys at school would love talking about pouring ketchup and mustard on other people. If we have current events this week, I might bring it up.

Camp count = $13.25 (Nana gave me a dollar today.)

Wednesday, June 12

Nana likes President Kennedy, so we watched him give a speech last night. Today, I read about it in the newspaper. The speech was about equal rights for Negro people. Two people – James Hood and Vivian Malone – wanted to attend the University of Alabama, but the governor, George Wallace, tried to keep them out because they are Negroes. A judge had already said they could go because they were qualified. President Kennedy said he was going to send Congress a civil rights bill so all people would have equal treatment.

Last January, when George Wallace was sworn in as Alabama's governor, he made the news for saying, "Segregation today! Segregation tomorrow! Segregation forever!" How can he think that way? He sounds like the Ku Klux Klan and that Bull Connor guy.

The newspaper had some of President Kennedy's important statements:

1. "Every American should enjoy the privilege of being American without worrying about skin color." *I agree.*
2. "Americans who do nothing to help are part of the problem." *Why does he think that? I don't agree; I haven't done anything wrong.*
3. "We are one country. Everyone should have an equal chance to succeed. All children should have the chance to be educated to the best of their own abilities." *I definitely agree with this one.*

At the end of the speech, the President asked for the support of all citizens. He doesn't just mean adults; he means kids, too. What am I supposed to do? I watch TV, read *Time* magazine and sit through sermons at church. None of the civil rights incidents happen in my town. I feel bad about what's going on in the South, but I don't know any Negro people. Why am I part of the problem? Why is my family part of the problem? I don't know how we are supposed to solve a problem if we're not *responsible* for it.

BREAKING NEWS
Medgar Evers Murdered at Home

Thursday, June 13

Late last night Medgar Evers, a civil rights worker from Jackson, Mississippi, was murdered. Mr. Evers had a wife and three children, and he worked with the NAACP, the National Association for the Advancement of Colored People. He was killed as he walked up to his home. I just can't imagine how horrible that is for his family and friends.

Someone said that when Medgar Evers was killed, he was carrying t-shirts that said, "Jim Crow Must Go." I wonder if the police will find the person who killed him; I hope they do but lately, sometimes the police help and sometimes, they don't. When these murders happen, usually the Ku Klux Klan has something to do with it.

Nana said she doesn't understand how people can be so terrible. She told me that all the hatred is a bottomless pit of grief. She is right.

Who *is* Jim Crow?

Friday, June 14

It's Flag Day, so the flag's up and I'm feeling patriotic once again. "Land of the free, home of the brave." Who are we talking about? Just white people? What does 'land of the free' mean anyways? Sometimes I wonder about the flag and patriotism when there's all this talk about who does and doesn't have freedom in this country.

Last Saturday at Girls' Friendly Society, we talked about the Children's Crusade. It would be great if we could just sit, eat our cookies and talk about GFS camp or favorite songs on the radio. Miss Simpson keeps reminding us about civil rights; she likes to talk with us about church and current events.

Sunday, June 16

Yesterday I spent the entire day babysitting at the church's Canterbury Market. I earned $9.00 taking care of little kids while their parents were busy at the Market. I am over halfway to my goal. *Yippee!*

It's Father's Day. After church Mom cooked a roast with potatoes around the pan for a special Sunday dinner. She made icebox cake for dessert, which is chocolate cake with whipped cream frosting served straight from the refrigerator.

Mom and Dad's three girls.

I made Dad a card and then I had a Father's Day problem. I didn't want to spend my camp money. So, Mom bought Dad a tie, and we all took credit for it.

Poor Dad. Later this week it's my parents' anniversary and then Dad's birthday is on June 21. He gets cheated out of presents because all his special days are close together.

Camp count = $22.25

Monday, June 17

Hooray! Last week of school! Next week, Judy comes to visit. Her mom will drive her down on Monday, and we'll take her back on Friday. It should be a wonderful week.

We got our Eighth Grade Required Reading book list today. We're supposed to read at least 25 books over the summer. Our school librarian suggests books for us. She told me to try these:

1. *A Wrinkle in Time*
2. *To Kill a Mockingbird*
3. *Island of the Blue Dolphins*
4. *Old Yeller*
5. *Johnny Tremain*

Nancy and I are going to whitewash the rocks that edge both sides of the driveway from the street to the garage. We get paid 30 cents an hour, so this will build my camp fund. Nana will give me another dollar soon. The only bad thing about whitewashing will be the bugs...but not the deer flies, because they don't get too close to the ground.

In *Time* today, there was a long story about Medgar Evers. I got sad all over again. It said he was a smart, nice man who was trying to do something good. He was actually *doing* something and trying to help – no, not help, more than help. He was supporting the civil rights movement. Medgar Evers was taking action with and for other people in his neighborhood, community and state to create a better life. He was working for "liberty and justice for all."

We don't have civil rights problems in our town and community. Maybe there are people here who are doing something, but I don't know who they are or what they are doing. Right now, in some ways it seems like there isn't any need for anyone to do anything here.

Tuesday, June 18

I don't understand the space race. Who cares if Russians get to the moon before the U.S.? We have lots of problems here in our country. We should just spend money on what's happening here and not worry about the moon. Most people disagree with me about the space race, including Dad. He thinks it's wonderful.

Anyway, on Sunday a Russian lady was launched into space. She's the first woman in space. I bet if we had been in school on launch day, we wouldn't have gotten dismissed to watch. She's Russian and female. Now the Russians are ahead of us. When Alan Shepard and John Glenn were launched, the teachers herded us into the dark gym and sat us down to watch it all happen on a tiny television. I was there but I couldn't see a thing.

If the U.S. needed a woman to go, no matter how much money they paid me, I wouldn't do it. They can just send the men. Or send the dogs and chimps, because they seem to do okay, too.

Wednesday, June 19

I am sitting on the front porch, leaning against the big column, thinking about tomorrow: the last day of school. Next fall, I'll be an eighth grader. It will be my second year in Weston Junior High School. Maybe then I won't feel so weird and left out.

Thursday, June 20

Today at school, we didn't do anything except watch the clock and yak. Some kids signed autograph books.

When I got home, Nana caught me up on the soaps because we'll watch together now that it's summer. We love to watch *As the World Turns* since one of the actors lives in our area. It's fun to look for famous people who live around Weston.

Friday, June 21

Happy Birthday, Dad! Another special meal – thanks to Mom and her chocolate layer cake. I made Dad laugh when I gave him a *picture* of a red sports car, which is what I'd really like to get him for his birthday. Everyone thought it was funny.

Sunday, June 23

Today at church, the kids with perfect Sunday school attendance got new books. Seventh graders got *Religions from Around the World*. It has information about the Jewish, Buddhist and Muslim religions and lots of other religions, too. In our family, we have Catholics, Methodists, and Christian Scientists, and we are the Episcopalians. Judy's family is Congregationalist, but they don't go to church all the time like we do. Mom's aunts are Christian Scientists, and they don't go to doctors. I wish we were Christian Scientists. I don't know why but I'm afraid of shots.

I won't write much with Judy here. She's coming tomorrow!

Monday, June 24

Judy arrived this morning. Her mom stayed for lunch and then returned to West Hartford. Mom made a fancy lunch and served it in the dining room. After her mom left, Judy and I played with Linda.

Judy and I carefully shared our diaries. She read first and it was interesting to listen to stories about her friends. No surprise she writes bunches almost every day. I read some of my entries but not the ones where I whine about her long, long letters. She liked the parts about *Time* magazine and Girls' Friendly Society. When I stopped reading, she said "Why don't you write this stuff to me?" I was surprised. I thought it would bore her.

Wednesday, June 26

Judy and I raced through chores this morning so we could go to Compo Beach in the afternoon. All the way over and back, Judy, Nancy and I sang to Linda. Linda loves it when we sing to her.

After dinner, we went to the Ice Cream Parlor in Westport. We had Tin Roof Sundaes and watched old movies in the nickelodeons. Dad gave us 50 cents each to buy penny candy, too. We like the button candies. It was a sweet end to a perfect day. Judy's staying one extra day because on Friday night, we are going to Chinatown for dinner and she's invited to come along. I've heard about chow mein, but I've never had Chinese food before.

Thursday, June 27

Judy's in the bathtub and I am going to write quickly. We spent the day fighting. I can't even say what we fought about. Dumb stuff. Sometimes she just doesn't make sense to me, and she gets whiney. I hear her getting out, so enough for today.

Friday, June 28

Judy was better today. We did a little babysitting for Mom while she took Nancy to her violin lesson. She gave each of us $1.00.

Camp count = $23.25

Saturday, June 29

Judy's parents came to pick her up and she was glad to go home. We had a nice time together, but we also had our not-so-good moments. Oh well.

Dinner last night was really something! Mom drove Nancy, Judy and me into New York City. We picked Dad up at his office and drove to a restaurant in Chinatown because we were invited to a special dinner. Dad has an office friend named Paul who is Chinese and who soon will be married to a Chinese woman named Betty. It's a little crazy but they don't use their Chinese names because they think it would be too hard for Americans to say. Anyway, they wanted to test their wedding menu on people who don't usually eat Chinese food. Paul chose Dad and our family to be the taste testers, and Dad asked Paul if it was okay to bring Judy, too. I don't think Judy was thrilled about eating Chinese food, but I was happy I wasn't stuck talking to Nancy the entire time.

At the restaurant we were seated in a private dining room upstairs with lots of red and gold Chinese designs and writing on the walls. Pictures and statues of Buddha covered the restaurant walls. Paul told us that Buddha has long ears to represent a long life. The table was round, and we were able to see each other as we ate. We were served so much food, one course after the other. At first, we tried to eat everything served, but Paul said, "There are twelve more courses, so slow down. Otherwise you won't be able to taste test it all."

There were 14 courses including lobster salad, roast pig, abalone, bird's nest soup, fried rice and noodles. Red bean soup and sweet lotus buns were served for dessert. Paul said there were lots of red foods because "red is the color of happiness." Before the first course was served, the waiters asked if we wanted to use chopsticks. I tried but didn't do too well, so I switched to a fork. Paul explained the meaning of each dish as it came. I never knew that food could have special meanings, other than birthday cakes. Different dishes stood for virtue, purity, wealth, happy marriage and peace.

After every course, Paul and Betty would say, "How did it taste? Should we serve this to our guests?" After dessert, the cook came out from the kitchen, we clapped, and everyone got a fortune cookie. I love my fortune: "Friendship doubles our joy and divides our grief."

We didn't have chow mein and no one even mentioned it. It doesn't matter, because the food was delicious...a meal I'll always remember. I wish that we kids were going to the wedding and the banquet afterwards, but only Mom and Dad are invited. I love Chinese food, but I wonder about Judy. She was very quiet.

Sunday, June 30

Summertime church seems long since we don't have choir, but short because we don't have Sunday school. Today there was another dose of civil rights because Dr. King had a Freedom Walk in Detroit, Michigan, so that was all over the news. Those civil rights people have stuff going on non-stop. Every day, everywhere civil rights is on the front page of everything including the TV. If "all men *really are created equal*," why are there all these problems? And, what about the women? At the rate we are going, I don't think there will be a time when everyone is free.

Mr. Greene always talks about civil rights because he says that "the church is the community that points out cracks in the world." There are lots of cracks in our country today. I'm not certain that anyone can fix them all.

There always seem to be cracks in the world. Anne Frank wrote in her diary about the world and all the dangers Jewish people faced. My diary seems more important when I write about the world outside of Merry Lane.

    During church coffee hour, my friend Vickie asked me if I wanted to go sailing next week. Sounds like fun.

July 1963

Tuesday, July 2

Yay! Aunt Bette is coming for the Fourth and we'll go to the beach all day and stay for fireworks.

I swept the garage and ironed today. Tomorrow, I am babysitting two little kids at church while their mom runs errands. I'll get paid 50 cents an hour. As usual at the beginning of the month, Nana donates to my camp fund. Today she gave me $1.25 and said, "You get a bonus for good behavior!"

I love reading my *Religions from Around the World* book. The religions can be so similar or different. Some have been around for a long, long time. Judaism has existed since 1300 BC. Buddhism started in India about 520 BC. Christianity began about 30 AD. It amazes me that two religions started in the United States. The Mormon Church began in New York in 1820, and the Christian Science religion was started in Massachusetts in 1879 by Mary Baker Eddy. Most religions have stories about a big flood and have only one God. So, I wonder, are we all praying to the same God?

There are different holy books for different religions.

Christians and Jews use the Old Testament. Christians also use the New Testament. Islam uses the Koran. Mary Baker Eddy wrote *Science and Health with Key to the Scriptures* and someplace in that book it says don't get shots.

The book also has information about atheists – people who don't believe in God. I know about them because I remember what happened when I was in fifth grade. Back then every morning after the Pledge of Allegiance, we sang either "America the Beautiful" or "My Country, 'Tis of Thee" and we said either the Lord's Prayer or the 23rd Psalm. Then an atheist lady named Mrs. Murray got a lawyer and sued so her sons didn't have to pray in school. The case went to the Supreme Court. She won, so no more praying in public schools. Everybody in every state got that new law.

Current camp count plus what I should make tomorrow = $26.75

Thursday, July 4

If there is sand in the diary, it is because I'm writing at the beach.

Dad cooked bacon and eggs for us at Compo Beach today. As we ate, sailboats moved into the Long Island Sound. It was a quiet, beautiful morning. After breakfast, we found a perfect spot for swimming and watching fireworks tonight. After lunch, Mom, Aunt Bette, Nana and Linda went home so Linda could take a nap; Mom and Aunt Bette fixed dinner and came back to the beach. Nana will babysit Linda. No fireworks for them.

Mobs of people are arriving, and we worried there wouldn't be a place for Mom to park when she returned. Dad's trying to save a space for her, so he put Linda's playpen in a parking spot. I'm supposed to be watching for her. Goody! Here's the car now.

Nancy, Aunt Bette, Mom, and me at Compo Beach on the Fourth of July.

Saturday, July 5

The fireworks were terrific, but I am so tired. The man who was in charge of the fireworks missed the train from New York City to Westport, so the fireworks show was delayed until almost 10:00. Yesterday was a long day in the sun. I still feel sticky from all the Coppertone sunburn stuff Mom slathered on me.

Sunday, July 6

At church today, I saw Vickie and her older brother, David. She said she didn't call about sailing last week because of the 4th of July. This week they are sailing and Vickie's going to invite me to come. I hope she doesn't forget.

My parents had a meeting at church this afternoon. I went and got paid $ 5.00 to babysit. I'm also doing odds and ends for Mom and Dad so that I can finish earning my GFS camp money. It takes forever at 30 cents an hour. Today, I also washed and cleaned out the car.

Current camp count = $ 32.00

Monday, July 8

There's a big long story in *Time* this week about the man accused of killing Medgar Evers. His name is Byron Beckwith. Some people were surprised about his arrest, but others weren't because he is a segregationist. And – of all things he attends an Episcopal church. It's awful to read that because it means someone from my church is a murderer. I wonder if he is a Ku Klux Klan member and wears those white sheets and frightening pointy hats to KKK meetings.

Tuesday, July 9

I went sailing with Vickie and Warren! We took the dinghy out to the boat, got the sail attached and went out, just a little way, into the Sound. We'd catch the wind one way, then duck our heads and turn the sail to catch it the other way. We even tipped over – I mean "capsized the Sunfish" – a few times. That's a little nerve-wracking at first, but then it's exciting. Once it's capsized, somebody has to stand on the dagger board to right it. That's a fun part of sailing.

Saturday, July 13

It's raining and I want to play Monopoly, but Nancy doesn't want to. She's buried in a book and won't come out. Why did I teach her to read? She learned when she was four years old when we'd play school at Ahmee and Grandpa Ray's house in California.

In 1958, just before we moved to Pennsylvania, Mom,

Nancy and I stayed with Ahmee and Grandpa in Encinitas, California, for six months. California was different. My grandparents lived on a high bluff across from the Pacific Ocean. At the end of the day I loved to watch from Ahmee's kitchen window where I could see the sun melt into the ocean. I went to Pacific View Elementary and learned about tetherball, tacos and vegetarians. I never saw a tetherball game until we moved out there. One day I bought school lunch and it tasted good, but I didn't know what I had eaten. When I got home Ahmee asked, "What did you have for lunch?" I described what I'd eaten. She got a big smile and said, "You ate your first taco." I didn't know about vegetarians until I met my teacher, Mrs. Halprin. She drank carrot juice every day for lunch. I remember thinking, I like carrots but I'm not drinking carrot juice.

Living with my grandparents was special for me. I loved swimming in the ocean with my grandmother. We would "float and bob, float and bob" just beyond the waves. I watched my grandfather fish and he taught me how to count to 10 in Spanish. We did a lot of sightseeing: the Point Loma Lighthouse, the San Diego Zoo and Tijuana, Mexico.

Every night before dinner it was "adult time," so no kids in the living room. It was "happy hour" for Nancy and me. We would go into our grandfather's study. I would sit at his desk and Nancy would sit at a TV table. I was the teacher, Nancy was the student, and during that school time, she learned to read.

I don't play school anymore, but I read to Linda and she loves it. I especially love reading Robert Louis Stevenson's *A Child's Garden of Verses*. I remember reading those poems to myself before I went to bed at night when I was little.

Sunday, July 14

At church, Mr. Greene talked about the March on Washington planned for next month. He said it is important for white people to support the civil rights movement, because "This is not just about the South. It's about everywhere in our country." When he said that it was *everywhere* in our country, I was confused. It seems like the demonstrations are just happening in the south. Mr. Greene said he is going, and he invited others to come, too. Mr. Greene said the reason for the March is to demonstrate that many people – Negroes and white people – understand that it's time for our country to change the way Negroes are treated. Our country needs more people, lots more people, to take action and promote change. It's time to turn away from segregation, time to embrace integration without fear. White and black people working, living and being together. Miss Simpson said she is going to the March on Washington. It's good but seems like a dangerous thing to do. How can a March on Washington change anything for Negro people? What difference can something like that make? I guess it's good if white people show up but what about when everyone goes home? Will everything be different?

Monday, July 15

All the Holiday House GFSers are getting ready. Since we leave Sunday, everyone's looking at the list of what we're supposed to bring. So much stuff: linens, personal items, clothes and, according to the miscellaneous part, not more than $10 for extra spending money. Who has $10 spending money? I just barely came up with my half of the camp costs.

We just finished school, but Mom is already thinking about next year's school clothes she's going to make us. Aggh! She wants to go to Yardage City to look at McCall's and Simplicity dress, skirt and blouse patterns. It takes so long to find patterns and look at fabric. We listen to Mom figure out loud right there in the store. It's as if she is trying to convince herself and us that it is going to work out.

It's not easy to match patterns and fabric and actually know what the two together will end up looking like. Mom knows but not me. It's easier to buy clothes at the store. But since I probably need more than one of each, Mom wants to make them. She can reuse the patterns on Nancy someday. Mom tries to make me feel better about shopping for patterns and fabric by saying, "Your clothes are 'one of a kind.'" I'm not sure that's a good thing.

Standing for the hem is the worst. Mom does all the cutting and sewing but not the hem. That's Nana's job.

Tuesday, July 16

Big news today! Current camp count = $33.75

Mom and Dad said they'd pay the rest, so I am all set! In five days, I am off to GFS camp with my friends. I can't believe it because I am so used to hearing the other kids at school talk about their camp experiences, ski trips and European vacations. I am especially jealous of the trips to Switzerland.

Wednesday, July 17

On the *Evening News* tonight, we heard about civil rights trouble in Maryland. Gwynn Oak Park, an amusement park near Baltimore, doesn't let Negroes in. Don't the owners want the money Negroes would pay? White people come on in. Negro people stay out. It's mind-boggling. I can go anywhere I want just if mom and dad say OK.

An Episcopal bishop was demonstrating with the protesters. It's good to know that an Episcopalian showed up; it seems like the Jewish people are always there. At first everything was calm; the demonstrators were singing and praying. Then bystanders got nasty. They were yelling, "n----r!" and "Send them to the zoo!" But instead of the mean, hateful troublemakers getting in trouble, the peaceful demonstrators got arrested. That's not fair. In school we talked about "freedom of speech" and that you can state your opinion if it doesn't hurt somebody else.

The bishop told a reporter, "These are my fellow citizens. Being able to go into the park is important to them and so it's important to me, too. The time has come. I must do something."

This reminds me of what President Kennedy said, that people who do nothing to help with the civil rights movement are part of the problem. Demonstrations are going on everywhere: Chicago, New Jersey, New York, and South Carolina. The NAACP criticized the President for not doing enough for the civil rights effort.

When our minister gives the sermon, it is mostly blah, blah, blah, blah, blah. I don't get much out of it until he starts talking about the civil rights movement. Then it it's hard not to listen because of the stories about real people.

Here we go again. The word "revolution" is everywhere on the TV and in the newspapers and I don't like it. I am getting used to the word demonstration, but I am not used to revolution yet. No matter what, I always think "I am so glad I don't live there; it isn't dangerous here."

Fair is fair. It will take forever before the news calms down and life isn't so difficult for Negro people. What will sermons will be like when the civil rights movement is over?

Friday, July 19

We went to the library today and checked out books. I'll finish them before I leave for camp.

We also stopped at church and I talked with Miss Simpson. She is excited about going to the March on Washington, but I am not excited for her. I am worried. What if it isn't a peaceful demonstration?

Saturday, July 20

Here I sit in my messy room with the door shut. I'm packing and stuff is all over. Mom is yelling and I'm trying to ignore her. After church tomorrow we leave for Holiday House and then I will write when I get home.

Postscript from Carol-Anne
2020

I think back to 1963 and now I understand that I lived a very contented and cozy life. I had my family, my home, my school. I participated in after-school activities that were fun – church choir, Girl Scouts, and GFS. I had special things to do like going to a play in New York City, sailing and summer camp. I never thought about it, but I lived a childhood that was safe, protected and isolated in many ways. I was very comfortable. I thought my life experience was what every kid my age experienced. And even though sometimes, I thought I had worries, I wasn't worried about people wanting to hurt me or my family because of the color of our skin. I now know that my worries were just typical teenage trials.

Why was it that way for me? I'm positive that I did not think about why it was that way for me when I was 13 years old – not even once. If I had wondered and thought about it, I believe I would have said that "I was so lucky."

I don't know when but at some point, I got a new and different idea. Maybe it was after I went to college and lived with three different black roommates – a girl from Guyana, a girl who was blind from Oakland, California and a girl who was an artist from Ethiopia. Maybe I got the new point of view after my parents told me stories about their family's "live-in maids" who were described as "members of the family." Violet and Inez cooked, cleaned house and cared for the children. They prepared the traditional family celebration meals but were not invited and included in those special occasions.

Today, I know that my childhood didn't happen because I was "lucky." It is complicated because it is about the history of our country. The quick answer is that it is about skin color, education and job opportunities. History tells us, however, that our democracy was founded by people who looked like my family and as a result, white people like me had opportunities for voting, education, jobs and much more.

What do you think?

Connecticut Crossings
August 1963

Saturday, August 3

Home. Still too tired and wound up to write, plus Mom is shouting at me to put my stuff away.

Monday, August 5

Finally! Camp was so much fun, and I can't wait to go back next summer! And guess what? No civil rights news for the entire time away! What a relief for me but I bet something is brewing somewhere in the South.

There were eight in our GFS group: Irene, Vickie, Kristina, Emily, Katie, Beth, Chrissie, and me. We stayed together on the top floor of the "Barn," which was for the older girls. Our room had six bunk beds. The bathroom was down the hall. We shared with four other girls, Leisi, Dani, Mandy, and Lesley. At Holiday House, "Ma" Strong was the housemother and Grace was the cook. Then there were all the counselors.

Every morning started with a flag ceremony. Then we had either a Morning Prayer or communion service that was held in the Chapel of the Transfiguration, which was a chicken coop that was "transfigured" into a chapel. Mr. Lakebee, the Episcopal minister led the services. On Thursday of our first week, he came out to Holiday House for the service, but no one was awake. Everyone in the whole camp overslept. He rang the chapel bell so we would "rise and shine" and get to chapel pronto. We raced around to get dressed and hurry to the chapel. I'm surprised he didn't gag from all the morning breath as he gave us communion.

On Sunday the counselors drove everyone to worship at Mr. Lakebee's church. The vans we took to town had "Girls' Friendly Society" written on the sides. I heard someone say, "Oh, here come those friendly girls!" It was kind of embarrassing.

After worship, we ate breakfast and enjoyed the activities. We always went swimming and did arts and crafts. We braided lanyards, made stuff with popsicle sticks, had archery, hiking, camp skills and nature talks. One of my favorite parts of camp was playing the piano in the Barn. For the first time ever, I went canoeing. I like canoeing almost as much as I like sailing. There was a little camp store that had candy and postcards. I bought a couple of postcards to send home and to Judy. Some girls had lots of money. Not me. Every evening we sang around a campfire. One night there was a talent show.

We ate our meals at the "House." We learned funny chants like, "Who stole the cookies from the cookie jar?" If you were caught with elbows on the table, everyone would chant, "Sarah, Sarah, young and able, get your elbows off the table! This is not a horse's stable, but a respectable dining table. Stand up, stand up, stand up and show us your face!" I almost wished that I would get caught. We learned new songs like "Kumbaya" and "White Coral Bells."

After lunch everyone would go to the mailroom. I was jealous of the girls who got letters. Some even got packages. Every day I hoped to get a letter from home and on the last Thursday, one finally came. There is something terrific about getting a letter from home when you are away.

Thursday morning, we hiked up Mount Canaan. It was hot. It was steep. I was miserable. I didn't really care to see the view at the top because I don't like heights. Some of the girls were in their glory. Not me. I couldn't wait to get a drink of water and get into the pool.

At the beginning of the week, I missed my family and home. I felt a little lonely for my own bed and everything I knew. One night when I was in bed and it was quiet, I almost cried, but the next morning camp seemed okay again, so I made it through.

Thursday, August 8

I forgot to mention the counselors. They are all so nice, but Jane is my favorite because she was the arts and crafts counselor. Everyone called her the Popsicle Queen because she always had a project that required popsicle sticks.

The overnight camp at Mohawk Mountain State Park was the first time I had ever done tent camping. There were ten of us plus three counselors. First, we had to put up this huge blue tent. Stakes, lines and tent poles had to be just so. After the tent was up, we did some hiking and bird watching.

We cooked our dinner over the campfire. Why does food always smell so good when it's cooked outside? Afterwards, we made s'mores and sang camp songs, and one of the counselors told ghost stories. I don't like ghost stories, so I just listened to the sound of the crickets and frogs, instead. Before bedtime, we had a few prayers and sang our GFS hymn.

On the last night of camp, we had a candlelight processional. Everyone got a small candle and we walked to the campfire singing:

This little light of mine, I'm gonna let it shine. This little light of mine, I'm gonna let it shine. This little light of mine, I'm gonna let it shine. Let it shine. Let it shine. Let it shine.

I was sad when Mom and Dad picked me up the next morning. But that night I was glad to be back in my own comfy bed.

Sunday, August 11

I am packing up again. This time I'm headed to West Hartford to see Judy. It'll be my first visit there. I won't take my diary because I don't want her to read that I said she is whiney.

Eight people from our church are going to the March on Washington. I bet their families are worried sick. All the Negro leaders are saying it is going to be a peaceful and dignified demonstration for freedom. Still, not all demonstrations end up peaceful.

Saturday, August 17

I am back from West Hartford and another terrific time. Judy lives in a real neighborhood, not out in the country like we do. She's lucky to live so close to everything and everybody. We walked to her school, her friend's house, and out to lunch.

At Judy's friend Candy's house, we sat on the back porch and listened to music. Candy had a record player that played 45s and LPs. We listened to the Four Seasons hits, "Sherry," "Big Girls Don't Cry" and "Walk Like a Man." We didn't just sit, we sang and danced. We probably looked ridiculous, like a bunch of weirdos, but it didn't matter. I really felt like a teenager that day.

On another day, we walked to Friendly's, which is a

restaurant and ice cream store. For the first time ever, I went out to lunch by myself with a friend. We each ate a hamburger and French fries, but what we were there for was the chocolate ice cream! Having lunch out was fun except for figuring out the tip. That's when I wished I was good at math.

One night, Judy's brother, Gregory, was home while Judy's parents went out. We were running through the sprinkler to cool down, and Gregory locked us out of the house. Judy got really angry. I didn't know what to think because I don't know Gregory. I couldn't tell if he was teasing or being mean. Judy finally persuaded him to let us in. She was going to tell her dad because then Gregory would get in more trouble than if she told her mom.

One really great thing about Judy's neighborhood was the ice cream truck. I remember those from New Jersey. Judy and I would be talking or watching TV and then she'd stop and say, "Is that the sweet sound of the Good Humor truck?" Then I'd hear the bells, too. We'd run around frantically to find change or get money from her parents before the truck got there. While we were running, we would laugh hysterically.

One day, her mom, Aunt Joan, dropped us off at the pool with our lunches. When we were ready to leave, we used the pay phone to make the 10-cent call for Judy's mom to pick us up. On another day, we went for a tour of Mark Twain's and Harriet Beecher Stowe's houses. We watched some TV and read books. Judy has the best suggestions for what books to read. We went to their huge public library. Judy tried to find *To Kill a Mockingbird*, but it was already checked out. She told me more about it, and I can't wait to read it now. I remember seeing the movie mentioned in *Time*, and it's on our summer reading list.

We only fought twice.

I really don't fight with Nancy, because Nancy gives up easily and goes back to reading whatever book she is reading.

But Judy? That's a different story. Although she gets whiney, she is smart and knows what she thinks and then tells me. She's good at it because she's had practice arguing with her brother.

Humdrum and The March on Washington
August 1963

Sunday, August 18

More news from the pulpit. Today, our minister talked about the March on Washington at the end of the month. He asked for prayers for the people from our church and everyone else who will be marching. Some people won't be saying the prayers he is thinking about.

Nana and I watched the *Evening News*, and they are calling it "The March on Washington for Jobs and Freedom." Many people worry it will get violent and hurt the civil rights movement. It's frightening – all the people they expect, the police, and all those *big* issues. My parents haven't said much, but they aren't going. I don't know what I would do if I were an adult.

Monday, August 19

Frances is back from her summer vacation in England. We

spent the morning blabbing at my house. We talked about our summers, and Mom let Frances stay for lunch. We timed it just right so that we went over to Frances's house for afternoon tea.

Our dining room is a sewing room disaster. So many projects. Nancy and I both have to try on clothes so Mom can get the waistband, the length and the placement of the buttons just right. It takes forever. And Mom must get it not "just right," but "perfect." There's lots of fussing about each garment. In the end, it really is perfect, but I think "just right" would do.

Wednesday, August 21

Days don't seem as lazy as they did three weeks ago. They get busier and "cranked up" as we get closer to school opening. *For heaven's sake!* There are almost three weeks before we go back to school. Today, after we got chores done and Mom did school sewing, we went to Compo Beach. I looked for Vickie and David, but they weren't around.

Mom is making me a new hunter-green corduroy jumper for church. The blouse will have a very light brown background with the same hunter green throughout. The fabric design reminds me of quilt squares – almost like the hex designs we used to see on Pennsylvania barns. I love it and I can't wait to wear it to church with my slip-ons.

Thursday, August 22

As school gets closer, I keep thinking that this year I want to find a real friend, someone like Judy, but someone who lives in Weston. A friend for more than one sleepover. Last year after Brooke's slumber party, it wasn't too long before she and Winnie quit talking to me. I even invited them both for an overnight. I was having a good time until they reminded me about Winnie's sleepover, the one without me. I have given up on both of them as friends.

Friday, August 23

Sunday is Nana's birthday, so tomorrow her sisters Kakie and Hon will show up. Nana and Hon share the same birthday, but they aren't twins. That's the way it is for Mom and Aunt Bette, too: sisters with the same birthdays, but not twins. Weird. We'll have a birthday party for the two sisters, and there will be lots of talking and laughing because they never agree on story details. Kakie and Hon will fight back and forth for the last word. Or Hon will interrupt Kakie with a one-liner and that stops everything. Then it's a free-for-all to get the conversation started all over again.

Both Kakie and Hon work just outside New York City in White Plains. Kakie is a manager at Saks where a lot of rich people shop. Hon has two jobs, at a bank and in the infant department at Lord and Taylor's. They talk about all the different people they meet at work. Some stories make me uncomfortable because we laugh at stuff that's kind of mean. I'm surprised they can eat and drink, because they are just constant with the conversation and silliness. It's better than a movie.

Saturday, August 24

Here I am with Nancy on the front porch waiting for Hon and Kakie to arrive for the birthday celebration. When Kakie's car pulls into the driveway, Nancy and I race to meet them because we know they come bearing gifts galore. They always bring "just a little something for the girls." That's us! I got a new blue madras blouse.

At the dinner table tonight, Hon had everyone laughing with a story about her job at Lord and Taylor's. She got a five-cent-an-hour raise because she did a great job of selling burp bibs to new mothers. Such a fancy store and they sell burp bibs! Five cents didn't sound like much to anyone but me. If you only earn 30 cents an hour, five cents sounds like a fortune.

Monday, August 26

It's quiet. My aunts went home yesterday.

Today it's really hot. I'm thinking about the people from church, especially Miss Simpson, heading to even hotter Washington, DC. The newspapers are covered with stories about Wednesday's March on Washington for Jobs and Freedom. The TV is non-stop about the organizers and everything leading up to the march. I've heard of some of the March people like Dr. Martin Luther King Jr., James Farmer, and Roy Wilkins. But who are Whitney Young, John Lewis, A. Philip Randolph and Bayard Rustin? There are stories about white church leaders who fight for equal rights. Negroes and lots of white people want civil rights legislation to pass in Congress. They want public schools integrated, no job discrimination, and everything fair for everyone.

President Kennedy thinks the March might hurt the chances of passing a civil rights bill. He's worried about possible violence. Me, too. We don't need more violence.

Many people want to attend the March on Washington but for whatever reason can't, so they participate in other ways. Some church volunteers from New York worked for two days to make 80,000 cheese sandwich bag lunches. Marchers also get an apple and a slice of pound cake. People in charge are telling the marchers to drink lots of water. The Washington Senators postponed their baseball games this week. Leaders of the March think 100,000 people might show up at 9:00 Wednesday morning and be on their way home by the end of the day. How on earth will DC be ready for so many people and keep everyone safe?

Wednesday, August 28

I watched TV from Nana's bed all day. I wanted to see if Miss Simpson or Mr. Greene would be shown, but that was ridiculous because of the huge crowd of people in DC.

All morning long, TV stations showed pictures of people, people and more people. They rode trains, buses and planes to get to Washington. One person roller skated from Chicago. He wore a sandwich sign that said "Freedom." People were lined up for miles along Constitution and Independence Avenues from the Washington Monument to the Lincoln Memorial. People carried American flags or signs that said "Integrate Schools Now! Equality! Justice! Freedom Now!" Negro men and women looked like they were dressed for church. It wasn't a riot. It was organized, busy, and peaceful.

Chicago to Washington, D.C., equals 700 miles.

At church last Sunday, Billy Greene, the minister's kid, sold 25-cent "March on Washington" buttons. Too bad I didn't buy one.

Thursday, August 29

Not so quick an entry today because there's so much to say about the March. I bet anything I'll be studying it in 8th grade American history class next year. I am going to get ahead, use Mom's Royal typewriter, and write up notes. I can use this for an extra credit report in English if not history. I'm usually not this organized.

Today I want to stay out of hot water with Mom because yesterday I spent most of the day begging her to let me watch TV and talking my way out of my chores.

March on Washington Notes

1. The March on Washington is important. Soap operas and game shows were cancelled. The *Evening News*, morning news and newspapers were filled with March on Washington stories.
2. Famous Negro and white movie stars were together at the march (Paul Newman, Joanne Woodward, Harry Belafonte, and Sidney Poitier). Paul Newman and Joanne Woodward are stars who live in Westport. Harry Belafonte sings calypso music. Sidney Poitier was in the movie *A Raisin in the Sun*. We read that play in school and the book had pictures of him in it.
3. Over 200,000 not-so-famous people marched, including people from our church; over 60,000 white people participated.
4. At the Lincoln Memorial, people held hands and sang "We Shall Overcome."
5. Some people sang "Ain't Gonna Let Nobody Turn Me 'Round." That song sounds like people take one step, and another and another. They were just walking, walking, walking with pride toward freedom.
6. At 9:30, the entertainment began. Joan Baez sang "We Shall Overcome" and Peter, Paul, and Mary sang "Blowin' in the Wind." (Kids sing those songs on the school bus!)
7. It was hot. Just before noon, even though the March organizers weren't ready, the crowd moved closer to the Lincoln Memorial. The organizers were trying to meet with U.S. Senators and Representatives on Capitol Hill.

They raced to catch up with all the demonstrators.
8. It was calm and safe.
9. About 2:00, the program began. It took forever because each speaker had a special story to tell. Marian Anderson was supposed to sing the "Star Spangled Banner," but her plane was late, so another lady sang.
10. There were many speakers and prayers. The newspaper listed the speakers. Here are some of the things they said and some of my ideas.
    a. Philip Randolph, the first speaker, said, "The civil rights movement is not confined to Negroes or to civil rights. Our white allies know that they cannot be free while we are not." *(What does it mean if I am free and someone else is not?)*
    b. Rev. Eugene Blake said that churches in the U.S. might have said the right things, but they didn't do the right things to help integrate society. *(That reminded me of what President Kennedy when he said everyone is responsible.)*
    c. There was a "Tribute to Negro Women Freedom Fighters." Mrs. Medgar Evers was supposed to speak but she didn't. Instead, the Arkansas NAACP director, Mrs. Daisy Bates, the lady who supported the Little Rock Nine desegregate Little Rock Central High School, introduced the other Negro Women Freedom Fighters. *(I was seven and I remember seeing photos of high school kids trying to go to school. Why is it that integration always has something to do with kids wanting to do something normal like go shopping or to school? Civil rights stuff has been happening for my entire life.)*
    d. Rosa Parks was introduced, and she said, "It's a wonderful day. Thank you." *(Rosa Parks is the woman who refused to give up her bus seat to a white*

person in Montgomery, Alabama. I remember that, too. Why would there be rules – no, laws – that said Negro people had to give their seats to white people?)

11. John Lewis had to change his speech because it was too stern, but still he said something about "burn Jim Crow to the ground." *(Who is Jim Crow?)*
12. Roy Wilkins announced that a leader in the movement, Dr. W.E.B. DuBois, had just died. *(Who was he?)*
13. Somebody read a speech that James Farmer wrote. He couldn't be there because he was in jail in Louisiana for disturbing the peace. He said that peaceful demonstrations would not stop until "our kids have enough to eat and are not cramped in Jim Crow schools." *(Is James Farmer really a troublemaker or was he jailed for no good reason?)*
14. Mahalia Jackson, the "Queen of Gospel," was all dressed up with gloves and a fancy hat. She sang a song about being 'buked and scorned. One newscaster said that Martin Luther King Jr. asked her to sing that song.
15. When Marian Anderson finally got there, she sang "He's Got the Whole World in His Hands."
16. Dr. Martin Luther King Jr., the best speaker, was last. He said, "all men are created equal" and "let freedom ring" and he kept saying, "I have a dream. I have a dream." His dream is the dream every parent would want for their own child. It's what I want for myself and for my sisters, too.

I'm glad I wrote those notes. Even with the typos, they'll come in handy.

Friday, August 30

Honestly, I thought I'd be bored with the March and all the speakers. It's not boring listening to people talk about freedom, democracy and injustice. I agree with the person who said, "Freedom is worth talking about." All the speakers were good, but Dr. Martin Luther King Jr. was the best. There was something different about the way he gave his speech. I had to listen to each and every word he said. I have never had an experience like that before, and I bet I never will again.

When he was finished speaking, the crowd exploded in cheers. I looked at the people on the TV and they seemed awestruck by what he had said. Some people were smiling, some were crying. I felt the same way. His voice and his message could not be ignored. By the end, even though I wasn't there, I had some tears streaming down my face, too.

Postscript from Carol-Anne
2020

When I was growing up Time *magazine, newspapers and the TV were full of troublesome news about civil rights. Even though civil rights was headline news I can't remember lots of conversations.*

Sometimes at school civil rights was a "current events" story. Even though in eighth grade social studies, we studied "American history" we didn't talk about civil rights issues such as Rosa Parks, Jim Crow laws or voting rights for non-white people. Maybe those issues were in textbooks, but I can't remember talking about them.

Sometimes, I had a short talk with my mom or dad. A perfect time to talk with my family would have been at dinner time. But dinner table talk was usually about homework and family stuff – not civil rights.

In church, except for very short GFS meetings, I listened to the minister talk about civil rights, but I don't remember having regular conversations about what was said. It was a start though because it got me thinking.

Maybe the adults I knew and saw everyday just were not interested in the civil rights movement. I remember my dad telling me that I was "too young to know what I think." Maybe my parents and teachers thought I was too young to have a serious conversation about this important issue. Everyone I knew was white. That might be why I didn't hear too much talk about civil rights. Maybe the adults in my life thought that the civil rights movement didn't affect me or my family because we are white, and we are nice people. We didn't live in the south and we would be kind to black people if they lived in our community. Perhaps the white people I knew thought it was enough to go to church on Sunday and pray for wise leaders who could lead us to a more calm and peaceful life for all people in this democracy. As I reflect now, I think that some of the adults I knew were probably challenged by the civil rights ideas and so they avoided talking about it.

In 1963, I understood about "what's fair." I realized that the civil rights movement and especially The March on Washington was a call for "liberty and justice for all" Americans – a call for fairness. Now, over fifty years later, our country is still working towards "liberty and justice for all."

I think most kids understand about what's fair and what's not fair. "Liberty and justice for all" is about fairness. Have you ever felt that something was not fair? Maybe you weren't treated fairly or perhaps you thought that someone you know, or some group of people were not treated fairly. Words and actions can be unfair. Some words frightened me because they don't encourage and promote fairness in our country: segregation, the Ku Klux Klan and white supremacy.

I watched the civil rights movement unfold before me in 1963; I remember feeling a little guilty that I wasn't doing anything to support the movement although I'm not sure what I could have done. My parents and my teachers didn't seem to have any ideas for me. The minister at church talked about the civil rights movement regularly but other than attend the March on Washington, he didn't have ideas about what I could do to participate in the civil rights movement. I knew that life wasn't fair for black people and I watched from a protected distance. I thought a lot about the issues, but I really didn't do anything to promote positive change in my community.

What do you think? Can kids do anything to encourage change in their communities? Can kids do anything to encourage a more peaceful community, country and world?

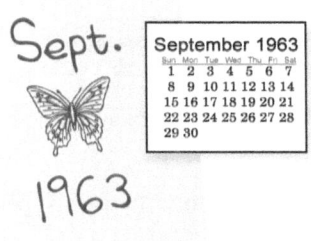

Interruptions and Special Announcements
September 1963

Monday, September 2

It's Labor Day today so Dad is home, and the flag is up. Mom's in the kitchen boiling potatoes for potato salad.

I owe Judy a letter, so I better finish the one I started. Sometimes it is harder to find a stamp and get the letter into the mailbox than it is to write it.

Tuesday, September 3

Time came today, and most of the issue was about the March. One article described it as "dignified" and said that the "thousands of marching Negroes were able to accept the responsibilities of first-class citizenship." Another article talked about the "beginning of a dream." I would never describe anything about the civil rights articles as funny but there was one silly comment about the "nitwit American

Nazi party" who was protesting the March. I am surprised they can print that.

In the "Milestones" portion of the magazine, it mentioned that William Edward Burghardt DuBois died the night before the March. He was a famous Negro, but I had never heard of him before this week. He died in Ghana. I don't even know where that is, but it's not in the U.S. *Time* said that Dr. DuBois started the NAACP and *Crisis*, a magazine for Negro people. It said he was a "card-carrying Communist." He was born in the U.S., but if he was a Communist, can he still be an American?

Thursday, September 5

September should be called birthday month. It's Linda's birthday next Tuesday and two days later, it will be Mom and Aunt Bette's shared birthday.

Today, our local newspaper, the *Weston Town Crier*, had pictures of families coming back from their summer vacations. They don't print photos of families like ours just coming back from Compo Beach. My mom is too busy sewing our school clothes to go on vacation.

Tuesday, September 10

My baby sister turned three! She got a tricycle but since there aren't any other little kids and no sidewalks on our street, she'll just have to bump along on our gravel driveway. The poor thing doesn't have little kid playmates except for when she's in the church nursery. We made a big fuss over her today, but when school starts, I wonder if her days get lonely? Nana's her only playmate.

Today was spent ironing clothes and getting ready for school. Mom's almost finished with her sewing projects. Nana has two more hems to do. Last week we went shopping for new penny loafers and lunch boxes. Mom packs our lunch, usually PB&J sandwiches. I wish for strawberry jam. Sometimes Mom packs peanut butter and pickle but it grosses me out because the wax paper gets soggy. We also get crackers, or if we are lucky, potato chips and a couple of cookies.

Nana's going to take Nancy and me to the gift shop this afternoon to buy Mom's birthday present and a card for Aunt Bette. I'll have to get Linda to sign, but she always writes huge and crooked and ruins the card.

Today in Birmingham (some people call it "Bombingham"), the schools were supposed to integrate but President Kennedy had to send National Guardsmen down there so it would actually happen. A lot goes on in Birmingham because so many white people don't like Negro people. I wonder if they go to church and hear the same kind of Bible verses and sermons I hear. It probably would be great if all Christians did "love they neighbor as thyself."

I finished reading *Uncle Tom's Cabin* by Harriet Beecher Stowe. Hey, Harriet! I've been to your house, and you lived just around the corner from Mark Twain. Were you friends? Did you two talk about books like Judy and me?

Uncle Tom's Cabin was hard to read. I was surprised that Stowe used the words "mammy" and "pickaninny." I guess those words were acceptable back then, but not now. I'd be a real ditz if I used those words. They are so disrespectful and unkind. I'm not sure how I know, but I do.

The school librarian told me that when Abraham Lincoln met Harriet Beecher Stowe, he said, "So, you are the lady who wrote the book that started this Great War!"

It's amazing to think that her book was almost as popular as the Bible back then.

Wednesday, September 11

Last day of summer vacation and I tried to do nothing. It didn't work too well because Mom wants everything to be ready for school. And perfect, of course.

I made Mom's birthday cake today since tomorrow is full of school and choir. Nancy wanted to help but I really wanted to do it myself because, after all, it's part of my present to Mom. I said, "You lick the frosting bowl." But no, she was smart enough to figure that one out. She said she wanted to put the frosting on, and she was making such a whiney fuss. So, I said, "Okay, you do it." Then, when she went upstairs to read, I fixed the frosting just the way I wanted.

It was a beautiful day today, perfect for being outside. After we got the cake made, I asked Nancy to come play jacks with me. She didn't want to because she is reading *Little House on the Prairie*, but I begged and pleaded and she finally said, "After the next chapter." I was willing to wait. We have the best spot for playing jacks, right on the front porch. It's a smooth, even space. It's one game we can play just for fun since there really isn't any room for cheating. Sometimes, Nana will play with us. She says she played a lot of jacks in her day.

Thursday, September 12

I lived through the first day of eighth grade. I hope it will be better than seventh grade.

The school subjects are the same: English, math, science, history, geography, French, Home Ec, and the dreaded PE. The kids seemed about the same, just one year older. From what I overheard, they are still busy with their huge allowances, shopping trips for store-bought clothes and trips to exotic places like Germany or the Swiss Alps.

Even though it's Mom's birthday today, we did the usual

running around. That's what happens when it's your birthday and you're an adult. Mom picked us up from school. We got ice cream cones and went to choir practice. We always do the presents before dinner. Nancy and I gave Mom a trivet that says "Kissin' Don't Last – Cookin' Do." Nana got Mom a new blouse, and Dad gave Mom a charm.

Nancy and me on the front porch for the first day of eighth grade.

My grandmother, Ahmee, has a wonderful silver charm bracelet with all her children and grandchildren on it. First, there is a large silver disk that has a beautiful raised design and the words "Helen and Ray, June 16, 1922." Then there are three medium-sized silver disk-shaped charms, one for each of her children, Bob, Shirlee, and Van, with their birth dates. Finally, there are small silhouette charms, one for each grandchild: Dale, Debbie, Carol-Anne, Nancy, Linda, Janet, Tracy and Danny. I can remember sitting on Ahmee's lap as a little kid and just turning that bracelet around and around on her wrist. She would read the names off to me and tell me the birthdays.

Several years ago, for Christmas, Dad bought Mom a gold charm bracelet, with two charms: a champagne bottle to celebrate their engagement, and a marriage license book that opens with three pages in it. One page has their wedding date. One has their initials. The last one says, "I Love You." Since then, Mom has gotten other charms: one for Nancy and one for me. She has one that says, "Our Tenth." Today, she got her charm that says "Linda" on one side and "9-10-60" on the other. Mom always cries when she gets a new charm. You'd think she would get used to it. I love the gentle click-click-clicking sound of Mom's charms.

Saturday, September 14

We had our first GFS meeting of the year today. The girls who went to Holiday House yakked about all the camp fun – swimming, hiking, arts and crafts, singing and campfires – and they talked about going next year. Nancy didn't seem too anxious to go so maybe it will just be me again. I hope so.

Miss Simpson told us about the March on Washington. Just like everyone else in our church, I'm sure my parents were invited to go along but they never mentioned anything about it. I guess they couldn't go because Dad had to work, and Mom was busy with us kids. I remembered how scared I'd been for Miss Simson and the people who went from our church. I asked if she got one of those cheese sandwiches and she said no, she had her own. She looked pleased as she talked about that hot day. And now, I feel a little jealous that I hadn't made the trip with her and the other members of our church. The newspaper pictures showed some white kids who looked about my age walking with the marchers.

Miss Simpson said that people are calling Dr. King's speech the "I Have a Dream" speech. She told us that what he said that day was not what he had written down and planned to say. He got sidetracked because someone from behind him said, "Tell the people about your dream, Martin." So, Dr. King started to give part of the same speech he had already given in June at the Great March on Detroit. That's when he told about his dream that "all of God's children, black men and white men, Jews and Gentiles, Protestants and Catholics, will join hands and sing with Negroes in the spiritual of old: Free at last! Free at last! Thank God Almighty, we are free at last!"

Then Miss Simpson told us she was trying to set up a special slumber party for us this year. She was kind of mysterious about it even though all the girls were begging her to tell. "No," she said, "I need a few more plans in place before I share too much." We are dying of curiosity!

Aunt Bette came out from New York on Friday night for the last birthday celebration for a while. It wasn't a big deal, just leftover birthday cake.

Sunday, September 15

The day started off just fine. We went to church. Nancy and I sang in choir and attended Sunday school. We went to coffee hour in the Parish Hall, our same old routine. Nana and Bette put a pot roast in the oven while we were gone, and the house smelled wonderful. When we got home, they left for church.

We had the TV on, and just after 11:00, we heard, "We interrupt this program for this special announcement."

That "special announcement" always means brace yourself for really bad news. It was the worst yet. A bomb killed four girls at the Sixteenth Street Baptist Church in Birmingham this morning. Unbelievable. I think a white person murdered those four girls. The girls, Addie Mae Collins, Denise McNair, Carole Robertson and Cynthia Wesley, were at church this morning, just like me. They changed into their choir robes, just like me, and then they went to the restroom. They probably were fixing their hair, so they looked nice for church. While they were in the bathroom, a bomb went off and those four girls died. Addie Mae, Carole and Cynthia were 14 years old, just a little older than I am. Denise was 11 years old, just a little older than Nancy.

If I lived in Birmingham and I was a Negro, this could have been me and my sister. When will the killing stop?

BREAKING NEWS
Four Negro Girls Murdered.
White Girls Safe.

Monday, September 16

Just like the memories of the marchers, the police dogs, and the hoses, the pictures of the church bombing will always stay with me. The blast was so strong it shattered brick walls and blew out store windows across the street. It damaged cars. In addition to killing the four girls, 22 other people were hurt, including Addie Mae's younger sister, Sarah. She lost an eye in the explosion.

In addition to that horror, two Negro boys were killed. First, a policeman told a 16-year-old Negro boy named Johnny Robinson to stop and he didn't, so the policeman shot him dead. Any Negro boy would be scared to stop if a white Birmingham police officer told him to. Johnny Robinson probably knew that the police dogs had bitten and jumped all over the kids during the Children's Crusade. Like me, he probably saw the pictures in the newspapers and on TV, but he could have *known* some of the kids who got sprayed by the fire hoses. It might not be right that he didn't stop but it is perfectly understandable.

Later, a 13-year-old named Virgil Ware was killed. He was sitting on the handlebars of his brother's bike, and they passed two white boys on a scooter with Confederate flags. Somehow one white boy shot Virgil dead. The kid with a gun was an Eagle Scout who'd been at a segregationist rally.

It's obvious that Ku Klux Klan people are responsible for these murders and this pain. I've seen the KKK pictures with men – maybe women too – dressed up in white sheets and pointed hoods, some of them holding Confederate flags. I've read about the burning crosses, the threats, and the lynchings. For some reason, the KKK hates all Negroes and Jewish people. They hate all Catholics and that means Nana. It's hard to believe and it doesn't make sense to me.

One KKK leader said the people who were responsible for the Sixteenth Street Baptist Church killings should "get a medal because children are white. Now there's just four less little n-----s." He's suggesting that Negro children aren't human beings which is terrible, absolutely appalling.

Yesterday's sermon at the Sixteenth Street Baptist Church was supposed to be "The Love That Forgives," but it wasn't given. That sermon was based on these Bible verses: "Ye have heard that it hath been said, Thou shalt love thy neighbor, and hate thine enemy. But I say unto you, Love your enemies, bless them that curse you, do good to them that hate you, and pray for them which despitefully use you, and persecute you."

I hear that message when I go to church and probably many other ministers preach the same message. I wonder if some white Christian people hear that message but forget when they're not in church. I remember a picture of a young Negro girl who carried a sign during the Children's Crusade. The sign said: "Can a man love God and hate his brother?"

I don't know if people can ever forgive something like this. I'm not even sure it's fair to expect that they could forgive or forget. I couldn't.

Wednesday, September 18

Today in Birmingham, funerals were held for those four girls. I don't know about the funerals for the boys, Johnny and Virgil, but I imagine their families are suffering as much as the girls' families. It's another "bottomless pit of grief."

Dr. King delivered the eulogy at the funeral service for Addie, Denise and Cynthia. I don't know why Carole Robertson had a separate funeral, but her family wanted it that way. Dr. King said the "girls would not die in vain." I wonder how comforting that message is for families and friends.

I keep remembering those girls were about the same ages as Nancy, Judy, my cousin, Debbie and me. How would our families feel if we'd been killed on a Sunday morning while we were combing our hair before singing in the church choir?

On Monday, Charles Morgan, a white man from Birmingham asked who did it. Then, he answered his own question by saying, "We all did it...every person in this community who has in any way contributed to the popularity of hatred is at least as guilty as the demented fool who set that bomb."

I think he got it right. I think he was talking about the white people.

Thursday, September 19

At choir today, we said a prayer for the murdered girls, the boys and their families, too. I am glad Miss Salinger had that idea.

There's a new girl at school who has the same English, math, science and PE classes that I do. Her name is Margaret Vernon. We walk to classes together. She doesn't have any friends and she probably needs at least one, just like me.

Friday, September 20

I finally had a chance to read *Time* magazine for the 13th of September. Nana said, "That Governor of Alabama is something else." When the schools opened and attempted to integrate, he tried to close them down. He bragged to newspaper people: "I want you to realize that there is not a single integrated school in the state of Alabama yet." That's not anything to brag about. That's just being heartless and stupid and then telling everyone about it.

At school, I found out about Jim Crow. Jim Crow is not a person but a law. It is a law that keeps Negro people from having the same kind of chances that white people have. For example, the Jim Crow law in Georgia said Rosa Parks had to sit at the back of the bus *and* give up her bus seat to a white person if all the other seats were taken. Another law in Georgia said that Negro and white people could not play cards, checkers, or dominoes together *and* that it was unlawful for a white baseball team to play on any field or baseball diamond that was near a Negro playground. My guess is that Alabama Governor Wallace knows all about Jim Crow but really doesn't care.

Sunday, September 22

The news is all bad. There's civil rights stuff going on all over the place in our country. Other countries are having problems, too. Almost everybody everywhere has big troubles and fighting goes along with it. Then the news people report it on television and radio, and in the newspapers and magazines. I wish everyone could be nice, behave, and get along.

Switching gears, as Mom would say, every once in a while, something's said about the Confederate flag. In *Time* last week, it said some people waved the Confederate flag when the schools were being integrated in Alabama. How ridiculous is that? Haven't they heard about Abraham Lincoln? The Civil War is over and has been for 100 years. This is the *United* States of America. What's taking them so long to get caught up with what's real?

We had a new boy in Sunday school today. His name is Scott.

Tuesday, September 24

Nancy drives me crazy when she practices her squeaky violin. Mom doesn't mind because she's so proud that Nancy's learning. Nancy is supposed to practice 30 minutes every day. Mom doesn't even have to remind her. Nancy has her own little corner in the living room with a special shelf for her music and a new music stand. It's Nancy's violin and no one is supposed to touch it except Nancy. She's already talking about the Christmas concert and playing a solo at Thanksgiving for Ahmee, Grandpa Ray and the rest of the family. She'll be center stage in November. It's not fair that I have to put up with the torture of listening to her practice, and she will get all the praise.

And, talk about unfair, today the famous poet Robert Frost came to her classroom and read poetry to her class – just her class. I can't believe it. Robert Frost wrote a poem for President Kennedy's inauguration two years ago. A few of his poems are in our eighth grade literature book. I love his poetry! Why did he go to Nancy's class and not visit the older kids who could appreciate him more, like me? Anyway, she told us all about it at dinner. He sat in the teacher's chair at the front while the kids sat on the floor. Nancy said his hands were wrinkly and old. He read several poems, and she said she could tell he really, really liked reading aloud. Her favorite poem was the one about the two roads in the yellow wood. I know that poem backward and forward. I memorized it for Mr. Bowman's English class. Why couldn't I have heard him read it?

Then Dad told us he had Robert Frost as a professor when he went to Amherst College. I didn't even know Dad went to college. Robert Frost was Dad's English teacher, but apparently, he liked teaching English about as much as Dad liked studying English. Neither one of them showed up for class very often.

Dad, did you know it's terrible to let an opportunity like that pass by?

Wednesday, September 25

Girl Scouts today, and the new girl, Margaret, joined our troop. We have classes together and now, Girl Scouts, too. I'm glad.

I am getting to know Margaret better. She is easy to talk with. We eat lunch together and have no trouble finding topics of conversation. Mostly we laugh at our own jokes and stories. Margaret has a brother who is older and four little sisters.

We got a postcard from Ahmee today from Taiwan. Ahmee said there is a surprise ahead for us because they "bought presents for the granddaughters."

Thursday, September 26

At choir, Scott, the new boy from Sunday school, was assigned to sit next to me. Big news: he isn't shorter than me! I wonder if he will be a regular at choir practice and Sunday school or if he just came today. He's kind of cute.

Saturday, September 28

We had GFS today and we planned projects for the fall, a food drive around Thanksgiving and a collection for the Red Cross. With the Red Cross, if you bring a nickel, you can get a pin to show that you donated.

Vickie brought Oreos for our snack, which everyone was untwisting happily when Janice brought up the four girls in Birmingham. Everyone got sad and sorry. Right after the bombing I had those girls on my mind a lot, but I'd forgotten for a while and I was really enjoying the Oreos. Miss Simpson suggested we take a collection and send it to Birmingham to support those families and the civil rights effort there. We all agreed that would be good to do.

Miss Simpson didn't say anything about the mystery sleepover she mentioned before.

Sunday, September 29

Today for church, I wore the hunter green jumper that Mom made for me. This outfit almost seems store bought to me. I don't want to brag or anything, but I feel so pretty when I wear it.

Monday, September 30

Time is covered with civil rights movement news. The cover story is about Governor George Wallace. His picture is on the front, and the article says Governor Wallace is smart. Well, he might be smart but that doesn't mean he's good. He is a segregationist, and, to me, that means he has no heart. I wonder how he feels about the kids who died on September 15. I wouldn't want him for my dad.

I got a letter from Judy today and she didn't write about Candy or Jillian or what's going on in school. She wrote about the church bombing in Birmingham and the girls who were killed, and isn't it awful? She was thinking the same thoughts I was: girls murdered and just our ages.

Postscript from Carol-Anne
2020

The civil rights movement captured my interest. Pictures in the newspaper and on TV terrified me because time and time again photos showed white people attacking black people. It was obvious that many white people hated black people and that hatred was seen every day in the newspaper and on TV. I understand now that many white people did not want to give black people a fair chance at freedom and the "American dream." Perhaps those white people felt that in giving black people a "fair chance" they would lose their own opportunities.

I watched TV and read Time magazine and thought "it can't get worse" but time and time again, it did get worse and it was never over. But I didn't worry for myself. I knew that that cruelty and brutality couldn't happen to me. I was safe and protected then, just like I am now.

Has anything changed since 1963? Has life improved for people who are not white? I'm not sure and to be honest, I'm not the right person to ask. I am sure, however, that we aren't where we need to be yet because when I look at the daily newspaper, civil rights issues – such as race, "dreamers" and immigration as well as voting rights – are front page news. There is still plenty of work to be done if our country really believes in and wants "liberty and justice for all."

I know that civil rights issues are important issues. In 1963 I didn't fully understand how very important civil rights issues are. In fact, I really didn't know much about civil rights because as a 13-year-old, I watched from a safe space as an observer. I wasn't really involved. Today, I remember times when I was an "on-looker" who said and did nothing. I feel embarrassed about those times now.

People from my church understood that life was not fair for black people and so, they marched in Washington while I watched TV. Over the years, I've met other adults who were my age at that time, and they showed up – they were at the March on Washington. I regret not being there.

In 1963, if I had thought and taken the time, I might have wondered what I could do. Today, I know that there are many ways to help and support, and not always, but many times, it is very easy to just by saying something or doing something. President Kennedy said, "One person can make a difference; everyone should try." I think that comment inspired me to want to do something.

I know that – even now – I have much to learn. I need to be a good listener which means that not only do I hear what someone says, I also try to understand what that person is trying to communicate to me. To really understand what someone is saying and *thinking, I must try to "walk in her – or his – shoes" and be open to different ideas and life experiences.*

These still are good ideas for me to think about today. The need for "liberty and justice for all" continues to be great. Sometimes I choose to contribute in small ways; sometimes I contribute in more significant ways. These are choices everyone – in fact, anyone – can make.

New Possibilities and Ideas
October 1963

Thursday, October 3

Yippee! I wanted a best friend in 8th grade and here comes Margaret up from Georgia! She talks with an adorable Southern drawl. I wish I sounded that cute. Margaret is almost as tall as I am so that's one really great thing about her. I am a little jealous that her mom lets her have long hair. Why won't mine?

Margaret is nice and so funny. Every day when we eat lunch, if someone wants to sit with us, fine. If nobody does, that's fine, too, because we have lots to talk about – sisters, parents, boys, records, Girl Scouts and other places we have lived. We also talk about dance class because her mom signed her up!

Margaret loves puns and she makes them up all the time. I told her she was the queen of puns and she said, "That's funny. I'm not from Punsylvania, you are." It doesn't matter what we are talking about, she can get a pun worked in and that cracks me up. I am getting better at puns, but I'm not as good as she is and probably never will be.

Margaret said she is going to invite me for a sleepover sometime, and Mom said I could invite her over, too. Mom has spoken to Margaret's mom, and we're going to carpool to dance class.

Friday, October 4

When Nana came to live with us, Mom asked if I wanted the huge mahogany four-poster bed that used to be Nana and Granddaddy's. I sure did. As I sit here and look around my bedroom with the white wallpaper with the big bouquets of violets, I feel pretty lucky. I love that I can shut the door and be by myself with no little sisters or parents bothering me. I'm glad I don't have to share my room like poor Nancy. She shares with Linda. Anyway, I am supposed to have my light off, but I thought I'd make a quick entry in my diary.

Tonight, was dance class. On the way there, Margaret and I talked about who we hoped to dance with even though we don't think of those boys as possible boyfriends. Margaret came up with a great idea. She called it the "Maybe So List," which has the names of the boys we wouldn't mind dancing with. Billy Beboe is not on the "Maybe So List." He is short and squirrelly. And, after we both said how we dread dancing with him, we both had to. I danced longer with Billy than Margaret did and when I was dancing with him, I couldn't look at her. For one thing, I really had to concentrate on my feet and for another, if I had looked at her, she would have made me laugh. Even though I didn't want to dance with

Here's Margaret!

Billy Beboe, I don't want to be laughing at him when he's standing right there. I'd rather have a good laugh later. I had to concentrate on not looking at Margaret and I could tell she was working at catching my eye.

When dance class was over and we were walking to the car, Margaret started teasing me about dancing with Billy. She was laughing and talking and carrying on with that lovely Southern drawl that seemed louder than normal. I was trying to hurry her along so that once I started laughing it would be in the car and not within earshot of Billy. He probably wasn't paying attention to us, but just in case it makes it much easier to laugh and be silly when you don't have to look out for the person you're laughing about. Still, it's great to have Margaret for a friend. Even though there's lots I don't like about dance class, with Margaret there it is more fun.

Monday, October 7

It is early in the school year, and I can tell math is going to be a major challenge, but since Mrs. Herbert is my teacher again this year, I know she will get me through. Sometimes I feel lost when she is explaining something, so I have a hard time paying attention and then I start to daydream. Mrs. Herbert will say "work through the struggle" and that seems to get me back on track. I'm jealous of my sister Nancy because math seems easy for her.

Tonight, Dad tried to convince me that math is fun. He took out his slide rule to show me how it works. I watched as he slid the gadget back and forth. It made no sense to me. His final comment was something like "Did you know that NASA mathematicians use slide rules? Their slide rules will land the first man on the moon."

No, I didn't know that, Dad.

Wednesday, October 9

Girls Scouts today. We are planning a fall cookout at Compo Beach. With a campfire, good eats and Margaret there, it should be a fun time.

I just got around to *Time* magazine today and the "Religion" section was about churches and the civil rights movement. Hundreds of members of the clergy took part in the March on Washington, including "two Roman Catholic archbishops, at least 10 Episcopal bishops and about 50 rabbis." I'm proud of the Episcopalians. The article said that since early 1963, over 200 ministers, priests and pastors have been arrested as they took part in picket lines and demonstrations. It sounds like it was good to get arrested. I wonder how all those congregations feel about their ministers being put in jail.

The article said, "So far, the white churches of the U.S. have been followers rather than leaders in the civil rights struggle." It's surprising, especially if they've been preaching "love thy neighbor." President Kennedy might agree, because last summer he asked everyone to do something to make things better.

In another article, two civil rights leaders disagreed. Dr. King said Negro people and white civil rights supporters should boycott Christmas gift buying to remind others, especially shop owners, of the six children who were killed in Birmingham last month. Roy Wilkins, head of the NAACP, said, "I find it difficult to go against Santa." I agree with Roy Wilkins. What does Santa have to do with the civil rights movement? It's weird two civil rights leaders disagree about this. I thought all Negro people would see eye to eye on those kinds of issues.

Thursday, October 10

At choir practice, Scott and I talked between practicing

the hymns and anthems. Miss Salinger didn't notice and now I have something more interesting to write to Judy about.

In the "Milestones" section of *Time* this week I read that Lyman Beecher Stowe died in Fairfield, which is 10 miles from here. Hmmm, haven't I heard that name before? Well, of course: he's the grandson of Harriet Beecher Stowe. I've been in his grandmother's house and read her book and I was practically neighbors with him.

Saturday, October 12

At GFS, Miss Simpson finally explained about the mysterious slumber party. There is a Girls' Friendly Society group in New York City, and Miss Simpson wants us to invite them for a weekend. All the girls were thrilled and cheered. When Miss Simpson said, "Of course, you realize that some, maybe all, of the girls are Negro," it got quiet. That gave us something to think about, so nobody said anything. Then Janice said, "It doesn't matter. It'll be fun."

It would be a new experience for all of us and there were many questions. What would we do? Would the girls like us? Would we like them? What if we didn't? Miss Simpson just kept answering the questions. She was sure it would be a great time. We decided to give it a try. Miss Simpson said the New York GFSers could come November 16–17. When Nancy and I got home from church, we asked our parents if we could be a host family and they said "yes."

Sunday, October 13

I sat next to Scott in choir. Today, we wrote notes during the sermon and we sat next to each other in Sunday school. I can't wait for Thursday.

Nana left today for White Plains. Every year, for about three months, she goes to work at Saks. She likes being with her sisters, but we miss her and the candy in her top bureau drawer. Nana says, "Christmas is more fun if I work," which really means presents galore, but I'd rather play cards with her at dinnertime.

Monday, October 14

In *Time* this week there's a story about Mrs. Kennedy's trip to Greece, the parties and the cruise. Jackie Kennedy is as close to an American princess as you can get. She has a sister who really *is* a princess.

We got a postcard from Egypt. My grandparents, our world travelers, saw the pyramids and the Sphinx. Next stop? Greece and Italy.

There's a story in the newspaper about voter registration in Maryland. Maryland isn't that far south. White people can register to vote but Negro people can't. Some folks are fussing because they don't want to change so it's fair for everyone. There is always something about the civil rights movement. There's no getting away from it.

Wednesday, October 16

Mom was sick, so no Girl Scouts today.

Report cards are coming soon. It's not that I do poorly but I don't do so well that there really is something to *shout about* and celebrate. I get some C's on my card with some B's thrown in. My parents don't pay me or Nancy for our grades like some kids' parents do. Nancy sails along in all her classes, no problems.

Thursday, October 17

At choir practice, Scott and I were talking until Miss Salinger yelled at us, "You two really need to try singing instead of talking." I was embarrassed. Mom was late picking me and

Nancy up, so Scott and I talked more. Then when I left, he said, "See you Sunday." *Yippee!*

I have to write Judy. She is shorter than me and blond and she's always writing me about her boyfriends. Now I can tell her about Scott.

Friday, October 18

The cookout was fun. It was chilly on the beach. We cooked hot dogs over the fire, sang songs, and blabbed. We had hot chocolate and for dessert, we had banana boats: chocolate, plenty of marshmallows and a ripe banana. *YUM!*

Saturday, October 19

Today we began planning for our GFS visitors from New York City. Miss Simpson thinks there will be sixteen girls and two chaperones. Now we have to find places for everyone to stay. We can take girls at our house and so can Janice and Erna. Miss Simpson said we need at least one more host family. We had to think about transportation, food, worship, activities at the church and host homes. Miss Simpson made notes on a huge yellow pad. Mr. Greene came to our meeting and said he was excited about the GFS Slumber Party.

Sunday, October 20

My dad thinks he is so funny. When we drive to Cannondale, we come down a long hill. The road turns and runs parallel to a pond that always has ducks. When we see the ducks, Dad says, "The ducks are looking for Carol-Anne," which means that ducks have their butts in the air. It isn't that funny, but everyone laughs.

The best part of the morning was choir. Miss Salinger pairs up choir members by height for the processional so I got paired with Scott and we sit together in church. We sit together in Sunday school. The 8th grade Sunday school hayride is next month. We'll probably sit together then, too.

Tuesday, October 22

I don't just read the "People," "Milestones," "Cinema" and "Books" sections of *Time* anymore, I like reading most of it, sometimes even the cover story. When *Time* comes to the house, I find a quiet place to settle with Nana's crochet blanket wrapped around me and then read. In today's *Time*, I read "Civil Rights: Farce in Birmingham." The police botched the case against the three men arrested for the Sixteenth Street Baptist Church bombing and the murder of those four girls. The article said, "Without sufficient evidence of the bombing, [Governor] Wallace's officials settled for a charge of illegally possessing dynamite, a misdemeanor which is about as common as jaywalking in many a U.S. city." In Alabama, people can kill kids and get away with it.

There's also a story about the Mormon Church not letting Negroes become priests. I just skimmed this article. Less than 1% of the population in Utah is Negro. Only two Negro people attend Brigham Young University. I wonder how those two students feel. I would feel *so* out of place.

Wednesday, October 23

Can't wait – choir practice tomorrow. I love singing and being in the choir but I really, really like seeing and talking with Scott. Who cares if we get in trouble?

A letter from Judy showed up today and it is seven whole pages long. *Ahhh.* I'll have to write a long one this time. Last summer, she said she liked what I wrote in my diary. I'll just copy some of my diary right into my letter! She'll never know the difference. Then, I'll fill in with the Scott update, and that should easily fill up the pages. Maybe I will even have more pages than she did. Now *that's* a happy thought.

Thursday, October 24

At choir, Scott asked for my telephone number and I gave it to him. If he does call, I'll beg Mom to let me take the call upstairs in the study off her bedroom so I can have some privacy. She'll probably say, "don't talk too long."

Friday, October 25

I am writing this before school. Margaret is staying overnight tonight. I hope Nancy doesn't bother us too much.

Saturday, October 26

Margaret and I had a terrific time together. We baked brownies and served them for dessert. We played Monopoly. We let Nancy play, but she got bored and went to find her most recent read. We watched some TV, but mostly we talked and talked until we couldn't talk any more. Margaret will be a friend even after this slumber party.

Plans for the GFS slumber party are about finished. We've got all the host families lined up, and other parents will help. Most activities will be at our church's Parish Hall, with everyone together. After dinner and a sing-along, we'll take our guests home. I'm excited but a little nervous, too. Every time I think of our visitors, I imagine them as black faces which reminds me of the faces of the choir girls from Sixteenth Street Baptist Church. I get sad all over again.

Tuesday, October 29

Boatloads of homework today. Especially math. In science, I have to do a report on the tape recorder, how it works and who invented it. I had to choose something from a list and that's all that was left. Dad will figure it out, explain it to me and then I type it on Mom's ancient Royal typewriter. Typing is slow and painful. I hunt for the letter I need, and then whack it. I need a sledgehammer to get the "b" key to go down. Good thing there isn't a "b" in "tape recorder." If I make a mistake – *arrrgh!* I have to type the page all over again.

Wednesday, October 30

With Nana gone, I'm babysitting Linda while my parents go to Open House at Nancy's school, Horace C. Hurlbutt Elementary. The boys love to say the name: Hurl-butt. Anyway, Nancy was excited because there's going to be a practice concert by the violin students. Nancy said she wanted to take Mom and Dad to the library attached to the fifth and sixth grade building. For Pete's sake, we go there all the time in the summer. I'm just happy I get paid to babysit Linda. Easy duty. She's been asleep since 7:30.

Scott called. It's the first time I ever talked on the phone to a boy. He talked about his family. His dad is an elementary school principal. He's the oldest kid in his family and he has one brother and two sisters. His sister, Sue, is a little older than Linda. Scott's a Boy Scout and when he goes to meetings, they play "War Ball" for the entire time. He loves that about Boy Scouts. Oh, brother. We girls earn Girl Scout badges and the boys are playing some dumb game.

Scott likes to play basketball and read archeology stuff. That sounds awful to me. We ended up talking for about 25 minutes until I heard our car pull into the garage.

BREAKING NEWS
Fire! Fire! Hurlbutt Elementary and Library Now Ashes

Thursday, October 31

We can't believe what happened last night. Nancy's school burned to the ground. Well, I should say, the fifth and sixth grade building and the Weston Public Library. It's horrible. It is probably the most shocking thing that has happened in Weston in ages. Who would think that a school would be there one day and gone the next?

The day started off normally. At breakfast Mom and Dad talked about the wonderful Open House and concert. They wanted to enjoy Nancy's event all over again. I was listening with one ear as I ate my oatmeal. Mom took Dad to the train station, and when she got back, just before we were about to go catch the bus, the telephone rang. It was Mrs. Allender, the room mother from Nancy's class. She told Mom that there was a huge fire at the school, and it had burned to the ground. No school today for fifth and sixth grade children. Mom quickly called the people on her class telephone tree. Nancy was as surprised as the rest of us, but she always takes news in stride. She asked a few questions and settled in for a day of reading and practicing her violin at home.

As I went out alone, I wondered where she'd go to school. I hoped they wouldn't find room at my school for fifth and sixth grade kids. And what about those kids who had class in the basement of the building, the kids who have some sort of problem like mental retardation or deafness? There's just about six or seven of them. Where would they go? Last night it was windy and rainy, but I didn't hear thunder. I didn't see lightning. How did the fire start?

The bus was noisier than ever until we slowly drove past the school. Firetrucks were still there, and it was still smoldering. Some jerky boy said he wished the junior high had burned down, too, and soon the other boys jumped right into that conversation with full agreement. Boys. They are so stupid sometimes. We have a brand new junior high.

After school, Mom knew more. She said she'd heard through the grapevine that someone threw a cigarette in the trash in the girls' bathroom, maybe a mom at Open House. She also said the Catholic or Congregational churches in town might let the kids go to school there. The Rabbi from Temple Israel congregation in Westport had offered space. The parents thought it best for the fifth and sixth grade kids to stay in Weston. But I was secretly happy no one's mentioning putting those little kids in my school. They're still deciding, which means Nancy gets another day off.

I almost forgot. It's Halloween. There are only five houses on our street. No one comes to our door and since I'm thirteen, I guess it doesn't matter anyways – I'm too old for Halloween.

Postscript from Carol-Anne
2020

Some of my earliest memories include attending church on Sunday; I never knew anything else. I thought every family went to church on Sunday. But I was wrong! I was, in a way, isolated from the real truth. I didn't learn the truth until I read a book about religions around the world.

In that book I learned that what I believed was not necessarily what everyone else believed. It explained that there were many similarities as well as differences between the different religions. That was a huge "wake up call" for me because it seemed to me that life would be so much easier if everyone thought just like me!

Now, almost every day it seems that I must re-examine my own ideas. I get new information and it isn't easy, but I re-think the old, more comfortable idea.

Have you ever heard something or read something that made you think you might be wrong about an idea you have? How did that make you feel? What do you think about new ideas?

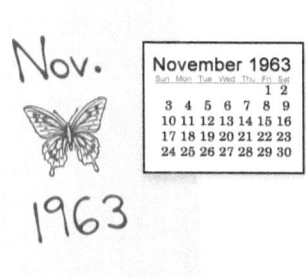

Sleepover and Sadness
November 1963

Friday, November 1

Mom got the call early this afternoon. On Monday Nancy will go to school at Temple Israel in Westport. For some reason, nothing worked out with churches here in our town.

Imagine! Nancy's going to school in a Jewish temple – a synagogue. Mom said the Rabbi called the school offices before the fire was fully extinguished. He's invited the parents and their children to see where they would have school. A kind of second "Open House" for the fifth and sixth grade families. I bet no one will be careless with cigarettes this time.

Ballroom dance class tonight. Margaret and I are taking bets on who has to dance the longest with Billy Beboe. I told her "I had him for the longest time last month. Now it's your turn." She didn't have a pun but she did say, "I'll be side-stepping that Beboe-boy before long." Oh, that Margaret. She's always got something to say.

Back from dance class. They tried to teach us the cha-cha.

Who does the cha-cha? Nobody, unless they are at ballroom dancing class at Weston Junior High School. Kids our age want to do the Twist, the Locomotion and the Mashed Potato. They only teach those if we are "good" during the first portion of class time. Then at the very end they let us do one of those dances.

Saturday, November 2

A picture postcard of the Parthenon came today. Ahmee and Grandpa Ray were in Greece and might be in Italy now. When I read about far away countries in school, they hardly seem real. Before too long, my grandparents will be here for Thanksgiving and Nancy's concert.

Sunday, November 3

At church today I saw Scott. I think about Scott when I am at ballroom dance class; I wish I was dancing with him. I can tell he likes me. He goes to school in Wilton, so I only see him on Thursdays and Sundays. Next week is the eighth-grade hayride.

Plans for the GFS slumber party are finalized. Miss Simpson spoke with the New York City GFS leader, Mrs. Baker.

At about 11:00, families with station wagons will pick the GFSers up at the train station. Our family has that duty. Back at church, we'll have games to get to know each other. Miss Simpson said we are responsible for one game and the NYC GFSers for another. We'll eat lunch and have some other activities – singing, board games, decorating the Parish Hall for Sunday coffee hour so church members know what we have been up to, and finally, pulling taffy. It sounds like great fun. Some parents will cook dinner for us. Then we'll have an evening prayer service and sing-along before we go home. Two girls and two chaperones will be staying at our house.

Today in church I passed a note to Scott that said, "I want to listen to the sermon" because it was about the civil rights movement. Mr. Greene talked about the need for all Americans to be treated fairly and with respect, no matter their color. My ears perked up because he mentioned that our GFS group was hosting GFSers from New York City. I wondered if our little slumber party might help some grownups get over old-fashioned ideas about white people and Negro people being together. It is just a small step, but is it a start?

Monday, November 4

Nancy and Mom talked about Nancy's school being at Temple Israel. After I got on the bus, Mom and Linda took Nancy to Westport. Rabbi Rubenstein welcomed the families and explained how everything would work. He said the school kids would not experience Jewish religious services or education. I bet that was important to the parents because I don't know of any Jewish kids at our school. He told them that at the end of each day, teachers and children would have to put everything away so the classrooms would be ready for the synagogue's regular after-school programs. Nancy said the room was a big space with dividers for the different classes. They didn't have books yet, but the teachers said books would come soon. Nancy was excited about going to school there. Teachers talked with the kids about taking good care of the building and being good guests. That's not a problem for *my* sister.

Fortunately, Nancy didn't lose anything in the fire other than her schoolbooks. Unlike me, she always remembers to bring everything home with her. She's already cutting up grocery bags for new book covers, for protection. We use grocery bags so we can collect autographs or just draw pictures on the cover.

Tuesday, November 5

It's Election Day today but nobody pays attention because we aren't electing a new president. It's just state and local people. It does mess up the evening television schedule because the newscasters try to keep up on who is winning or losing.

Wednesday, November 6

Girl Scouts today. I am working on my last badges needed for First Class Scout. Almost done!

Recently, Judy's letters have had a cookie theme and she's been bragging about all the cookies she's made. Aunt Joan lets her bake cookies or brownies whenever she wants. Judy's got a mile-long list of all the cookies she is planning on making. I think she copied the table of contents out of some cookbook. They sound delicious but I hope I don't have to read the step-by-step details of every recipe she tries out. Mom is the queen of her kitchen. She doesn't want me or Nana cooking in it. Since Nana doesn't know how to cook, it makes sense to keep her out of the kitchen. But me? I'd like to learn.

Thursday, November 7

Scott wasn't at choir practice today, so it wasn't as interesting.

It's been a little over one week since the school fire, so life has settled down. Nancy says, "School is school. Everything's the same except it's a different building with a longer bus ride." Nobody's said anything about where the special kids from the basement classroom are going to school. Even though there's just a few of them, I guess they still have to go to school.

My parents told us that Uncle Van is getting married next month in Knoxville, Tennessee. Dad's the best man, and the four of us are going. I've never been to a wedding. We'll travel through some new states for me – Virginia, Maryland and Tennessee. Plus, Mom and Dad said we'll drive through Washington, D.C. on the way home. If we have time, we might tour a plantation. Ever since I read *Gone with the Wind*, I've wanted to see one. Our cousins Dale and Debbie will be in Knoxville, too. Should be fun but with all the civil rights unrest, I'm a little nervous.

Friday, November 8

Mom bought fabric for a skirt for the Christmas dance. She talked with Margaret's mother and they have an idea they are going to work on. This is one of those times when Mom has a plan, and I don't have any idea of what she is thinking. I have to wait to see how things finally end up. She said not to worry because this idea is "perfect." Sometimes just hearing that makes me worry.

Saturday, November 9

Our GFS group is ready for the New York City GFSers. We all have some sort of responsibility. We made welcome posters to put around the Parish Hall. Miss Simpson is going to make copies of the weekend schedule so everyone knows when events begin and end. I hope everything goes well. With all the civil rights movement upset and tension, it would be wonderful if this little joint effort went smoothly. When I think of those four girls who died in Birmingham, I feel so unhappy. I wonder how our GFS visitors think and feel about it or if it will come up. It seems like we're trying to do something good by just having a sleepover. So maybe there is no need to talk about that sad topic. The President said those who do nothing are part of the problem. At least this is something.

Eighth grade cookout and hayride tomorrow. I can't wait!

Sunday, November 10

Church and choir were fine. The cookout was fine, but the hayride was a disaster.

The cookout started off okay. At 5:00, twelve of us eighth graders met at the church. Vickie's parents and Miss Simpson had the grill lit and we fixed our own hot dogs. Kids brought something to share. I took Mom's potato salad. After dinner, we made s'mores. Then it was time for the hayride. It was a cool, bright evening. We piled into the station wagons and rode out to the hayride place. Everybody was excited as we got onto the wagon, and I was happy because Scott sat right next to me. The moon was up. The stars were out. Some of the boys were stuffing hay down each other's backs. So immature. I was feeling grown up, especially when Scott reached over to hold my hand.

Then he leaned over and whispered to me "Why do you always wear that green dress to church? Is that the only one you have?" I was so shocked and ashamed. I yanked my hand back, changed seats and couldn't wait for the hayride to be over. All I wanted was to go home. Dad picked me up and asked me how it was, and I said "Fine." Dad didn't ask any more questions and I didn't say a thing. I just sat and watched out the window 'til we got home. I didn't have the energy to tell Mom and, anyway, *Ed Sullivan* didn't look interesting, so I just went to bed.

Monday, November 11

I told Margaret about the hayride and she rescued me from my misery. In fact, she came up with a terrific idea. Margaret is always making lists and she's got a new one, the BZ Boys List. Scott is at the top. BZ stands for Below Zero and she explained that's what Scott is worth. Margaret said we should add in the names of other worthless boys as they crop up. No doubt, they will. It is so great to have a friend like Margaret around.

Tuesday, November 12

I'm getting over the hayride but I'm wondering what's going to happen at all the choir and church services ahead. I wish I never had to see Scott again. I don't know why people must be mean. I'd like to think that Scott didn't know he was being mean. But he was. I will remember those two questions for the rest of my life. To be honest, when I go to church, I want to look my best. I have one really nice outfit, and I save it for Sundays and other special occasions. I didn't realize that Scott was just like the stuck-up kids at school. I don't care. Scott can concentrate on girls who go clothes shopping at Saks and Lord and Taylors. That way, I won't get in trouble at choir.

Wednesday, November 13

Postcard from Barcelona. Ahmee says they're counting the days 'til Thanksgiving. All the cousins and family will be here – three males and nine females at the table. Talk about "We Gather Together." The women do the work. The men carve the turkey and that's about it. If we're lucky, one of them might clean the big turkey pan. Grandpa Ray, Uncle Tommy and Dad go on and on about being outnumbered and try to make us feel sorry for them. But no one does because they really don't do any of the work.

Thursday, November 14

Before choir today, Margaret reminded me not to sit near or look at Scott. No problem. He had the same plan. I didn't say one word to him. Choir took forever, though. I just remembered he likes to spend his time playing War Ball. How stupid. Never mind. The GFS sleepover is on Saturday, and that's much more important. I am getting excited about it.

Sunday, November 17

It was a wonderful weekend. The New York GFS girls took the train home a couple of hours ago. Everything is still spic and span from all the work Mom made us do to get ready, so I'll just write until she calls us for dinner. She and Dad are buried in the Sunday papers. We had two girls stay over, Cheryl and Siri, plus Cheryl's mom, Mrs. Baker, and another lady, Mrs. Fowler. But I should start at the beginning.

Nancy and I got to the church at 10:00. Everything was almost ready. Some girls were finishing decorating the gourd and cattail centerpieces and setting the tables for lunch. I was having trouble getting our welcome poster taped up, and it had just fallen off again when the cars with our guests arrived from the Cannondale station. Janice said, "Let's just hold it up," so we did. We smiled and waved while the cars unloaded. It took a few minutes for the girls to find their bags and come inside. They were all Negro, but I was surprised that some were light-skinned, and some were very dark. A couple who were sisters wore matching red berets with their hair smooth and the ends turned under. Some girls had their hair done in braids with bows and barrettes sticking out from under their hats. How must we look to them, I wondered, with our pixie haircuts and ponytails? Every girl – Negro and white – was different but at the same time it seemed like there were similarities. Everyone was excited but nervous and quiet, too.

Mr. Greene welcomed everyone and said a prayer of thanks for the opportunity to build friendships during our time together. Miss Simpson took over directing everyone. We made name tags and got into the games. The games helped the ice melt, so it wasn't just the adults standing around talking.

Happy Birthday Party!

First, we partnered up and asked each other at least ten questions so we could introduce each other and say something interesting. I introduced Cheryl. Cheryl is twelve and just about my height, so we had something in common from the get-go. She has three brothers and one sister. She lives in an apartment building and has a parakeet named Bella. She is an alto and sings in her church choir, just like me.

The introductions were going along very politely until one of the visitors, Bonita, had her turn. She did a bang-up imitation of Ed Sullivan, hand gestures, accent and all. "We have a really big 'shoe' tonight and I want to introduce Miss Melinda Riley whose claim to fame is that she can do handsprings the length of this room." Those of us who knew Melinda knew this was not even close to the truth, so we burst out laughing, Melinda, too. By the time the games were over, everyone was chatting away with new friends. We talked about GFS meetings, what we did, our service projects, the songs we sang. Throughout the visit we sang GFS songs, campfire songs and hit songs from the radio. I saw Miss Simpson dab her eyes when we sang "This Little Light of Mine."

We also had an old-fashioned taffy pull. None of us had done this before, except Janice. Her mom worked in the church kitchen making sure the vat of boiling taffy was at the proper temperature for just the right number of minutes. She came out banging a pot to say it was ready, so we buttered our hands and took globs of hot brown taffy. I worked near Cheryl and her friends Bonita and Siri. The insides of their hands turned pink, like mine did, as we pulled and pulled our candy. Bonita took Siri's taffy and twisted it together with hers and the two girls pulled and stretched it far apart. She gave a little jump rope twirl and started, "I like coffee, I like tea..." We were laughing, but Mrs. Baker made us stop, cut the taffy into pieces and wrap it in waxed paper to send back with our guests. We all sneaked some tastes. Fantastic!

After supper when Mom drove us home, Nancy and I pointed out the Cannondale train station where Dad catches the train every weekday morning. They'd already seen it because that's where they arrived. Cheryl said, "It's dinky. You could get at least 50 little stations like that into Grand Central Station."

We drove over the bridge and up toward the junior high, Mom explained that Nancy's building had burned to the ground, so the kids were attending school in Westport at Temple Israel. "Was the fire set?" asked Mrs. Fowler. Mom told her, "No, it was a careless smoker on a windy night." Mrs. Fowler said, "Oh," and got quiet. I realized how many fires have been intentionally set in Negro communities – homes, churches and maybe even schools. The fire at Nancy's school was awful, but there wasn't the true horror of knowing some hate-filled person had set it. It was an accident.

Dad and Linda greeted us at home. We got the car unloaded and showed everyone where they were sleeping. Dad put a fire in the fireplace so the four of us (Nancy, Cheryl, Siri and me) sat in front and just watched. Siri showed us a picture of her little sister at a birthday party and gave Nancy and me a copy. She said, "My sister has her head tilted because she's so sassy." We heard the grown-ups in the kitchen fixing popcorn and talking about who knows what. The adults weren't having any trouble yakking up a storm. We girls ate our popcorn and talked too. We took the blankets and sheets Mom laid out for us and put together our own sleeping spots. I was a little self-conscious. Should I talk after lights out or not? It didn't matter; soon we were asleep.

This morning when we got to church, Miss Simpson was in the Parish Hall with donuts, orange juice and hot cocoa. The other girls arrived while we were eating. After the morning service and Sunday school, our new GFS friends caught a train home to New York City. But before they left, there were thank-yous all around and some hugs, too.

After church, Mom told me about the conversation she had with the chaperones in the kitchen. Mom described it as "rougher waters" because she had asked what they thought about school busing as a solution for school integration. Mrs. Baker was for it and Mrs. Fowler was completely against it. We were surprised there was disagreement.

When I found a quiet moment, I thought about our Sunday sermon which was a warm welcome to our new GFS friends; it focused on our good time together. Then, I began to wonder if the sermons our friends from New York hear are like what we hear every week – civil rights. I guess there are some big differences because some white people need to learn to be fairer to Negro people.

Ahmee sent me a postcard that shows a different world.

Monday, November 18

After a fun weekend with our visitors, I wondered if I would ever see those girls again. Usually, after visitors I have to write thank-you notes because it's one of my aunts bringing presents. Since it was such a good time, it felt as if I should write a thank-you note to Cheryl and Siri, even though we didn't really give each other gifts.

Tuesday, November 19

Margaret asked me to come over on Friday night and Mom said yes. Our moms are friends, too.

Another postcard from Ahmee and Grandpa, this time from Hong Kong, showing houseboats on a river. Mom says Ahmee hasn't been on that side of the world in ages. It's taken so long for the card to come you'd think it is missing the stamp. My grandparents will be here a week from tomorrow. My parents will go down to the dock to pick them up. It's the first time they have visited since we moved to Connecticut.

They certainly took the long route to get here.

Letter from Judy today. She spent five pages (two full sheets and another side of paper) telling me how awful Scott was and, "if that's your favorite outfit, you should just wear it any time you want." By the time she signed off, I was mad at Scott all over again.

Wednesday, November 20

At Girl Scouts today, Margaret and I spent time talking about Friday night and what we're going to do. We're fixing dinner for her family so we can finish the cooking badge for First Class. We'll talk about boys on our Maybe So list but that shouldn't take too long. Most boys are so goofy and immature, they end up on the BZ list.

Friday, November 22

I just want to stay home. I'm not going to Margaret's tonight. I am not watching TV. I'm in my room. Door shut and radio off. I bet I don't even listen to the radio for a week. A terrible thing happened today. President Kennedy was shot and killed.

During science class, Miss Maclean, the principal, came to the door, and Mrs. Kragthorpe went to speak with her. Then Mrs. Kragthorpe returned, looking strange. She told us, "early dismissal today" because the President had been shot. We all gasped. She didn't say anything else. Everyone went into shock. The hallways were quiet as we walked out to catch the busses home. Some kids were crying.

Then I saw Mom, Linda and Nancy waiting in the car. After I settled in, Mom said that President Kennedy had died. When Mom was returning from lunch with Nana in White Plains, traffic slowed way down and came to a complete halt. Police officers were trying to direct traffic, but nothing moved. Mom couldn't figure out what was happening. There was no accident. People were just sitting in their cars. Then she noticed some were sobbing. When she could, she asked a police officer, "What's going on?" He told her "President Kennedy has been shot, and it's just been reported that he died." Mom immediately decided to pick Nancy and me up from school. Texas Governor John Connolly was also shot but he's alive.

Saturday, November 23

On the news today, we learned the President's body has returned to the White House. The casket lies in the East Room, and there are two Catholic priests there. The family had a private Mass in the East Room. All day long, we listened to speeches on TV. There are many ways to describe the sorrow everyone feels, but at the same time, the words just aren't totally there. Listening and watching all this sadness – even when someone like the Chief Justice tries to make the best of it – wears me out.

We watched TV all day.

Lee Harvey Oswald was picked up for questioning. He's the main suspect. After President Kennedy was shot, there was mass confusion. Forty-five minutes later, Oswald was seen exiting the Texas School Book Depository building, the building the police think the shot came from that killed Kennedy. When Police Officer Tippet tried to stop and question Oswald, he was shot and killed.

Today the White House was the center of activity. Former Presidents Eisenhower and Truman came to pay their respects and many other government people showed up, too.

Nancy was sad, but she was disappointed because she missed Saturday morning cartoons. When she said that to Mom and Dad, they got so cross with her they sent her to her room. She's probably reading now. I wish I could.

Sunday, November 24

From Nana's loveseat I can look out her window and see the tops of the trees and the last of the fall colors in the late afternoon sun. They are a welcome relief. The TV is on and has been all day, but I turned the volume down. I heard Chief Justice Earl Warren speak. His message was clear: Americans come together when a President dies especially when it is a violent death. Warren said that the President reflects "the ideals of our people, the faith we have in our institutions and our belief in the fatherhood of God and the brotherhood of man." He believes that Kennedy was "a great and good President, the friend of all people of good will, a believer in the dignity and equality of all human beings." Dignity and equality. That's what it's all about these days.

Everything was cancelled today except for church. We prayed for the President's family – Mrs. Kennedy, Caroline and John-John, his parents, brothers, sisters and all the nieces and nephews. We prayed for the Tippet family. We prayed for our nation. Everyone needs prayers today.

Dad doesn't mind that both TVs have been on nonstop. It's all about the news right now, and it keeps coming. I was on the family room couch downstairs after lunch as Mom and Dad did dishes. They were talking quietly behind me. Suddenly, a real murder happened right on TV. A nightclub owner named Jack Ruby killed Lee Harvey Oswald, the man picked up for questioning about President Kennedy's murder. Never could I imagine that I'd witness a murder. It was on TV and in front of millions and millions of viewers, including me. What next?

Jack Ruby entered the Dallas police department building where Lee Harvey Oswald was held. He walked toward a group of men, including some police officers who were escorting Oswald to the county jail. Oswald was handcuffed; two men were standing right next to him. Ruby took a big step forward, pointed the gun at Oswald's side, and shot him. I saw Oswald grimace and fall. Once again, there was total confusion and chaos. I told my parents what I'd seen. They came over and were glued to the TV, too. Jack Ruby was arrested immediately.

I got teary when the newscasters broadcast live from Washington, D.C. We watched the horse drawn caisson go from the White House down Pennsylvania Avenue to the Capitol so the President's body could lie in state there. The casket passed lines of soldiers who carried the flags from 50 states. The only sounds heard were the drums and the horse hooves as they clopped against the hard pavement. It's as if the horses kept beat with the drums. It sounded so sad, lonely and hopeless.

Over and over all weekend, we watched the tape of last Friday in Dallas. The President and Mrs. Kennedy as they got off the plane and were greeted. Smiles and roses as they moved past the crowd and a cavalcade of cars going down the street. Then, shots and everything changed. The President slumped into Mrs. Kennedy's shoulder. She turned around to a Secret Service agent who was climbing onto the trunk at the back of the car. Later, we saw the new President – Lyndon B. Johnson – take the oath of office with Mrs. Kennedy standing right next to him. She had blood splattered all over her. Newscasters told us her suit was pink.

Today the President's body was taken from the White House to the Rotunda. Mrs. Kennedy and the children led the procession into the Capitol building. The new President Lyndon Johnson laid a wreath. Then Mrs. Kennedy and her daughter approached the casket and touched the flag that draped it. Mrs. Kennedy leaned forward to kiss the flag.

Such a long entry. Such unbelievable news. So much sadness the words just won't stop coming.

Monday, November 25

School was canceled today, just like everything else because of the President's funeral. Another day with eyes glued to the television and we watched every moment of it. It was so heartbreaking to see Mrs. Kennedy, Caroline and John-John. Newscasters reported that about 250,000 people waited patiently in line to pay their final respects to the President at the Rotunda. It's hard to imagine because the weather has been bitter cold.

At 10:00 this morning, both Houses of Congress passed resolutions expressing sorrow, a formality. One thing I learned over this weekend is there are many formalities that must happen. Certain rules or customs are always followed when there is an event of this sort. Senator Margaret Chase Smith from the state of Maine laid a single rose on the desk that Kennedy sat at when he was a Senator. That wasn't a custom or a formality. It's just what she wanted to do.

At about 11:00, President Kennedy's body was taken from the Capitol Rotunda to St. Matthew's Cathedral. Mrs. Kennedy was escorted to the funeral by the President's brothers, Senator Edward Kennedy and Attorney General Robert Kennedy. They walked in the freezing cold from the White House to the cathedral. Mrs. Kennedy was dressed in black, and a black veil covered her face. Her eyes looked straight ahead. It probably took every ounce of her courage to not collapse. The children rode in a car.

The crowd stood quietly as the caisson went slowly down the street, past government buildings and flags all at half-staff. Bells tolled; bagpipes played. On TV you could see people wiping tears away. We did on Merry Lane, too. At 12:00, there was a hush across the nation. Everything stopped for five minutes so the American people could pay their respects to the President.

After the funeral, the casket came down the front steps of the cathedral. Mrs. Kennedy leaned down to whisper something to her young son. That's when he saluted his father's coffin. Poor little kid. It was his third birthday. He's a baby just like Linda. And then the procession to Arlington National Cemetery and lighting the eternal flame. Finally, we turned off the TV. It was the longest single day of my life.

Tuesday, November 26

At school today it was talk, talk, and talk about everything that has happened since last Friday. In every class, it was the same. Talk, talk, and more talk. All the teachers suggested in one way or another that "life goes on. We'll move forward and keep going." That's just fine, but life seems very different now.

With all this weird, unreal stuff going on, I practically forgot Ahmee and Grandpa Ray will be here tomorrow. Dad won't go to work. He and Mom will meet their ship in Hoboken.

Wednesday, November 27

When we arrived home from school, Ahmee and Grandpa Ray were here. Getting them was complicated because the dock workers were on strike in Hoboken. My parents had a police escort to a room with a large window, and they watched for Ahmee and Grandpa get off the boat. Once the four of them were together, they watched as my grandparents' belongings were unloaded. The biggest crates were the presents for us granddaughters: carved camphor chests.

They are two feet tall and smell like medicine inside, the stuff Mom puts on our chests when we have a cold. I didn't know camphor was a kind of wood. Mom said the present is a hope chest – something a girl can put things in for when she is married and has her own home. The idea is okay, but I don't have anything to put inside other than some silver salad forks and spoons. No problem, because Mom seems eager to use mine and Nancy's.

A Camphor Chest – It's pretty, but it stinks!

I didn't realize it but while we watched the TV coverage of President Kennedy's funeral, Mom cooked ahead for Thanksgiving. Tonight, we had our traditional night-before-Thanksgiving meal: vegetable soup with yummy bread. Before dinner, Mom reminded Nancy and me that "children should be seen and not heard." What a dumb rule. How old do children have to be before they get to participate in "adult" conversations? When we sat down for dinner, Grandpa Ray said the table blessing. I had forgotten from our time in California what this meant. Once he gets going on all the food, people and things he's thankful for, it seems like he'll never stop, and we'll end up eating cold food.

Tomorrow, cousins Dale and Debbie come. When we are together, I spend most of my time with Dale. She is three years older than me but she's my type. She's quiet and likes to read. Debbie's just my age but she's such a tomboy, we don't have much in common. My aunt has a great garden, and she wanted my cousins to pose by her flowers. Debbie wouldn't. So, we have a picture on our mantle of Dale, every hair in place, by some rose bushes in full bloom and another picture of Debbie holding out two huge cucumbers like fish she just caught.

Thursday, November 28

Happy Thanksgiving! Too much going on to write!

Friday, November 29

It was a fantastic, funtastic Thanksgiving. We never ever had such a "mob" (Dad's word), but it was our mob, and it was super!

Nana and Aunt Bette arrived early, and Mom put them to work. Aunt Bette always makes the salad. Dad worked on the turkey. Nana finished up the dressing. Nancy, Ahmee and I set the two tables, the big one plus a kids' table. Everybody was busy...well, almost everybody. Grandpa Ray sat in Dad's big chair next to the fireplace. He enjoyed watching everybody else work.

After we set the tables, Ahmee wanted special time talking with the Merry Lane granddaughters before the New Jersey granddaughters showed up. Nancy and I watched as Linda sat on Ahmee's lap and played with her silver charm bracelet. "Where's my charm?" Linda asked as she turned the bracelet round and round. Ahmee showed her each charm, just as she had done for Nancy and me when we were little. At about 1:00, the rest of the family arrived, and food started to roll right out from the kitchen. We don't usually have appetizers on Thanksgiving Day, but yesterday we did. Aunt Shirlee brought her family famous "Shirlee's Cheese Crispies," and Mom contributed shrimp. For the first time ever, I ate shrimp. They were delicious. Just before the feast, Nancy took center stage with her violin. She played several pieces and, finally, "We Gather Together." That song was perfect for our family gathering but my cousin Debbie and I rolled our eyes toward heaven to keep from laughing.

Grandpa's prayer was so long, Mom had a challenge keeping Linda calm. The rest of the family just stood around and waited patiently. When Grandpa finally finished, everyone yelled "Amen!" We had normal Thanksgiving food including turkey, dressing and gravy, mashed potatoes, sweet potatoes with marshmallows, cranberries and Nana's cranberry salad (that's a recipe she can make), Aunt Bette's tossed salad, green peas, turnips, creamed onions, rolls, and pumpkin pie.

At dinner, the talk continued back and forth, on and on. It is fun to hear about Dad, Aunt Shirlee, Mom and Aunt Bette when they were little kids. There was lots of reminiscing between Nana and Ahmee because they are friends from way back. My grandparents knew each other when their children were very small. There were some new stories, too. We hooted when Ahmee told the story of her second cousin Dotty Dimple learning how to drive. Who would name a daughter Dotty Dimple? After we had eaten all that we possibly could, Nana passed around Whitman's chocolates. Even though we were all full to the brim, everyone had just a smidgen of room left for a chocolate candy.

Nana, Aunt Bette, and my cousins and their parents left about 6:00. The rest of us collapsed in front of the fireplace and talked about the day all over again. It was wonderful. I spent more time with Debbie this visit. Dale seemed older, more grown up. She wanted to be with the adults and chat with them. I listened for a while but then Debbie, Nancy and I went into the family room to play Clue. Debbie and I got a little silly, but that's okay. Family fun.

Saturday, November 30

We had a nice quiet family day today. No GFS and no extra company other than Ahmee and Grandpa. Tonight, was home movie night. Dad set up the screen and projector. We watched recent films and some older ones. We took turns providing the narration. Sometimes we didn't exactly agree, so there was a lot of talking over each other, which drives Mom crazy. Dad showed some of the movies he took when we were in California living with Ahmee and Grandpa. We saw the Point Loma Light House, the San Diego Zoo and swimming in Uncle Lester's pool. We saw movies about bringing Linda home from the hospital. I remember well. Nancy and I hurried home from the bus stop. We knew Mom and Linda would be there. Unfortunately, we got home before Dad had his camera ready, so he made us go back down the hill before we could see Mom and our new sister. Then he took movies of us running up and into the house all over again.

Postscript from Carol-Anne
2020

The year 1963 was nonstop sorrow and sadness because of the unrest and suffering of the civil rights movement and the assassination of President Kennedy. Most Americans were heart-broken. I was sad when I saw pictures of children especially black kids who were jailed, hurt or murdered. I was sad as I watched President Kennedy's young daughter and son stand with their mother at their father's funeral. While those lives played out in the headlines and on the TV, I sat comfortably on "the sidelines." It was as if I watched people and their stories pass by. I was very interested, but it wasn't something that touched me in a real way. It was someone else's life and story. I was removed from that other real world.

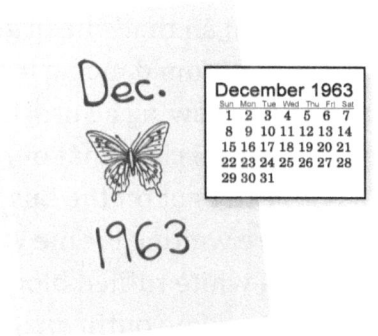

Dance Parties
December 1963

Sunday, December 1

It was a jam-packed ride to church today with seven of us in the car. Nancy and I sat in the way-way back of the station wagon, which was hard since I was all dressed up (in my favorite green jumper). Ahmee and Grandpa Ray enjoyed our service, and they especially liked seeing Nancy and me singing in the choir. After church we ate Ahmee's home-made coffee cake. It was a calm day, and everyone needed it. Tomorrow, my grandparents leave for New Jersey for their visit with Dale and Debbie. I'm sad they're leaving because it may be a long time before I see them again.

    I need to write to Judy. It's my last chance to write before stamps cost more. It's ridiculous. In January, a postcard will cost four cents and letters will cost five cents. Plus, we have to start using some stupid extra number called "Zip Code."

Tuesday, December 3

Dance class Friday. With all that's been going on, who could even think about ballroom dancing lessons? Margaret and I knew our moms were sewing a surprise for us. After school today it became crystal clear that our mothers were "in cahoots" on this project. I got off the bus at Margaret's house, and Mom was there waiting for me with a new bright red Christmas skirt and a white ruffled blouse. Margaret's mom, Mrs. Vernon, had the same outfit waiting for Margaret. Twins. The skirts are sort of okay: red with Christmassy borders at the hem. The material is thick, so the skirt sticks out funny, but Mom says it'll calm down. I'm not sure being twins is a good idea. Margaret agrees with me.

Wednesday, December 4

I didn't look at *Time* at first when it arrived this week. The whole issue is about President Kennedy's assassination. I can tell by skimming that it's more of everything we heard last week. Reading it would make me feel exhausted all over again.

The "People" section listed the royals who are pregnant. England has plenty of pregnant ladies including Queen Elizabeth and two other women I don't know, the Duchess of Kent and Princess Alexandra. The "People" section stuff is easy to read. This week I need that.

I'm going to have to get a new diary because I am running out of space. Who knew my life would be so interesting?

Thursday, December 5

School news.

In PE today, I overheard two girls talking about shoplifting. Rita and Glenda discussed where they shoplift and were bragging about passing out candy to their friends. I couldn't believe my ears. I didn't recognize the names of the stores where Rita shoplifts but Glenda likes to shoplift at the drugstore where Mom gets her cigarettes and we get ice cream cones on Thursdays. I told Mom what I heard, and she shook her head and said, "Not good."

On a happier note, in choir we are getting the special Christmas music ready. I love knowing all the words and singing both the soprano and alto parts. Singing favorite Christmas songs takes my mind off being near the number one person on the Boys' BZ list. I've noticed that he likes sitting near Paige. I don't care. She's a year younger than me and has tons of different dresses to wear on Sundays.

We're also getting music ready for the Christmas program at school. I should say "winter program." That's what they are calling it this year because they can't have a Christmas program at Temple Israel. The fifth and sixth grade kids will have a program, but the Rabbi thought it wouldn't be right to sing religious Christmas songs. I hadn't thought about that before, but it makes sense. It's part of being respectful and being good guests. Temple Israel isn't available in the evening, so the Winter Program is scheduled during the school day, which means that probably only the moms and younger brothers and sisters will be going.

Friday, December 6

Dance class tonight is billed as the "Christmas Party." Everything is about the same except we'll have nicer refreshments, something different from the regular store-bought cookies. Probably there will be ginger ale in the red Hawaiian Punch. All the girls will be dressed up in something special for the holiday. I'm excited to have a new outfit to wear for the Christmas dance but I'm nervous about being Margaret's twin. Mom and Mrs. Vernon put the finishing touches on the skirts today.

Saturday, December 7

The hour and a half I spent at dance class last night was the *worst* hour and a half of my entire life. It couldn't have been worse if I had to dance every dance with Billy Beboe. It was horrible for Margaret, too. The finishing touches did us in.

Last time we'd seen them, our skirts looked okay. The border patterns were a little different. I had holly berries and bells. Margaret had Christmas trees, snowmen and bells. But we looked like twins, fraternal twins, maybe. That was bad enough but that's not all. On Friday morning, while Margaret and I were at school, our mothers added small silver bells to the bottom of our skirts. After I got dressed, I told Mom my skirt was "noisy", and I felt weird in it. She pooh-poohed what I said and told me, "Margaret's skirt has bells, too. You'll be fine." I walked as quietly as I could out to the car and Dad.

Silver Jingle Bells are small, but loud!

When Margaret jingled into the car, she looked miserable, too. I could tell her mother had probably tried to cheer her up by saying, "Carol-Anne's skirt has bells, too. You'll be fine." On the way, Margaret and I discussed our dilemma. Movement, any movement, was a problem. Dad listened but didn't add his two cents worth until we arrived at school and just sat, not getting out of the car. When we still didn't get out when he held the door, he said "What makes you think you are so important that anyone is going to pay attention to you?"

So, we got out. As we walked towards the school cafeteria,

we knew we were in trouble. Somebody said, "What's that noise? Is Santa early this year?" Margaret and I hung up our long winter coats, stood for a minute and then made a beeline to sit down. Our skirts were louder than any orchestral bell section and there was *nothing* we could do to stifle the sound. Billy Beboe pointed and said, "Here come the jingle bell twins." I was so mortified, I wanted to die. Margaret did, too.

That was just the beginning. Margaret and I ting-a-linged throughout the entire dance class. The boys never stopped snickering. I'm *never* wearing that skirt again, even if Mom takes the bells off.

Sunday, December 8

I'm still angry at Mom for that stupid jingle bell skirt. I can't believe she thought that would be a good idea. Would she wear a skirt with bells? Probably not. I remember she had a skirt with a boxer dog on it with a leather leash for a belt. Would she have worn it if the dog barked? Dad got mad at me because Mom worked hard to make the skirt for me.

Another thought about that awful jingle bell skirt. After all the torture Mom put me through, she never said sorry. Maybe she didn't understand how miserable that dance class was for me. I guess she didn't because otherwise she would have apologized. Whenever I upset Nancy, my parents make me apologize. I say the words but don't really mean them. Mom must not know that trick.

So, I'm hiding out in my room because I want to be alone. Nancy's got a good idea. Read your worries away. In English, we've just been assigned *The Diary of Anne Frank*, so I better start re-reading that sad story. I skimmed it last time. This time, I'll pay better attention since I want to get a good grade on the book report.

Monday, December 9

Time was all about the new President, Lyndon Johnson. He spoke to Congress and said, "Let us put an end to the teaching and preaching of hate, evil and violence. Let us unite in those familiar and cherished words: 'America, America. God shed His grace on thee, And crown Thy good with brotherhood, from sea to shining sea.'"

There were articles about President Kennedy's funeral, Lee Harvey Oswald's funeral and Jack Ruby. It was interesting to read about Mrs. Kennedy and how she wanted the funeral to be like Abraham Lincoln's. She had the White House windows draped with black curtains throughout the mourning period. I read how Senator Kennedy told his parents the news. JFK's father is ill, so the decision was made to tell Rose Kennedy, the President's mother, first. She kept the secret until Senator Kennedy arrived the next day. That seems like a terrible secret to have to keep. They pretended the TV was broken so that JFK's father wouldn't find out from television coverage.

The North Portico White House Door is draped to show that the White House is in mourning.

Time listed some names of the 1,200 people who attended the funeral service. Martin Luther King Jr. got there late. Why? It seems that for something that important, you'd want to be sure to be on time.

Tuesday, December 10

At school today I looked at two magazines we don't get at home, *Life* and *Look*. The December 6 issue of *Life* said 6-year-old Caroline Kennedy told a playmate she "only cried twice." I wish my parents would get *Look* because it has the best pictures. On the cover of the December 3 edition of *Look* is a sweet picture of President Kennedy and his son John, and the cover story is "The President and His Son." The magazine went to press before President Kennedy was killed. So, here were all these happy pictures of a little boy and his daddy including photos of John-John sitting in his dad's rocking chair, hiding under the President's desk, walking hand-in-hand with his father. There were a couple of silly pictures including a pretend spanking and shared secrets. In one, John-John is saluting just like he did the day of his father's funeral. It broke my heart all over again.

Wednesday, December 11

I'm home sick from school today. Flu. I missed the math test. I don't like taking make-ups because it feels weird taking a test all by myself. When I take the test, Mrs. Herbert will tell me where to sit and say, "Just do your best, honey." That's about all any of us can do.

I'm enjoying *The Diary of Anne Frank* much more this time, probably because I have my own diary. Here's a quote from her diary that I read today: "Everyone has inside him a piece of good news. The good news is that you don't know how great you can be! How much you can love! What you can accomplish! And, what your potential is!" Really? Is it really true for everyone, Anne? I hope so. I have no idea what the assignment will be for *Anne Frank*, but I bet anything I can use that quote.

Friday, December 13

It's Friday the 13th and I'm not superstitious, but if I find an eyelash, I'll make a wish and send it on its way with my fingers crossed.

Our family has some silly family traditions. Now that I am a teenager, it seems stupid, but when I was younger, I loved this one. Now, Linda's the big fan. At the dinner table, after grace, my dad will smile and ask, "Who are we?" We all hold hands and say, "We're the Hughes!" I don't know how that got started. It was probably Dad's idea.

Another tradition Dad got started happens after we've eaten a big meal. The kitchen is finally cleaned up and, with everyone in earshot, Dad will shout, "Oh boy, am I hungry!" Then, he goes to the refrigerator and pulls out ice cream and asks, "Where's the chocolate sauce?" My mother gets so annoyed with him and yells, "Bob! No!" But nevertheless, he'll make a chocolate sundae for himself and for anyone else who wants one. When I was little, I'd eat a sundae with him, but I don't anymore. So, Dad gets aggravated and grumbles, "If we had boys around here, they would appreciate a good chocolate sundae when offered!" Too bad, Dad, you've got TWG, "Three Wonderful Girls," plus Mom, of course. (TWG are Dad's ham radio call letters.) Maybe someday if you get lucky you might get a grandson or two, but don't hold your breath.

Saturday, December 14

Today at GFS we talked a little bit about the sleepover with the girls from New York. So much has gone on since we had the sleepover it was hard to remember. We asked Miss Simpson if we would be going to visit those girls at their homes and she said, "We'll see but I don't think so because some people might think it could be dangerous." What? Do Siri, Cheryl, Bonita and the other girls live near dangerous places? That's scary. It's our last GFS meeting until January 1964. I can't believe it – 1964!

Everyone's busy with Christmas doings. Mom's baking and sewing up a storm. We know she's sewing while we're at school because there are little bits of thread on the floor, and we have to watch for pins that have fallen. Christmas cards are stacked on my camphor chest in the front hallway. Dad bought the wreath and tree today. Mom decorated the living room mantel and it looks terrific with greens, three little angels and the N-O-E-L candle holders in the center. Dad has fun changing them around to spell L-E-O-N or E-L-O-N.

Today, I looked back in my diary and noticed that I haven't written down the GFS prayer. I want to have it in the future. *"O Lord, our Heavenly Father, we beseech Thee to bless us and all who belong to the Girls' Friendly Society. Strengthen and protect us by Thy fatherly love and vouchsafe to us the guidance of Thy Holy Spirit. Help us all to bear one another's burdens and to live not for ourselves, but for others as members of one family in Christ. Cleanse us from our sins, make us holy by the indwelling of Thy Holy Spirit, and bring us all at last to the joy of Thy Heavenly Kingdom; through Jesus Christ, our Lord. Amen."*

I don't understand all the words, but I like the idea of being helpful to others and not being so selfish. After our get-together with the NYC Girls' Friendly girls, I like to think of them saying this prayer, too.

Mom took me shopping for Judy's present and I got her a cookie cookbook. I brought it home, wrapped it with Christmas wrap and then grocery bag paper. Mom's going to mail it Monday so it will get to West Hartford in plenty of time. That's a first for me.

Sunday December 15

Ahmee and Grandpa Ray are home in California. It's Grandpa's birthday today so we made a quick call. Nancy, Linda and I sang "Happy Birthday to You" while Dad held the phone.

Sometimes *Time* has a "Television" section. It lists special programs coming up, and last Friday night, I watched *The Bob Hope Comedy Special* because Peter, Paul, and Mary were on. They sang "If I Had a Hammer" and "Blowin' in the Wind" just like they did at the March on Washington. It's nice to have a bit of peace and calm after all the November misery.

Monday, December 16

Vacation begins Friday! Nana's coming home and Aunt Bette will be here, too. Right after Christmas, we go to Knoxville.

Time had an article about the people investigating the President's assassination. I wouldn't want to be on that committee. They'll have to re-live the entire event from start to finish over and over. It was bad enough seeing it unfold the first time.

The "Milestones" section announced a new royal baby in Sweden named Désirée Margarethe Victoria Louise Sybilla Katharina Maria. And I think *I've* got a terrible name.

Tuesday, December 17

I am excited about Uncle Van's wedding. My cousins will be there. This trip will be my first time in "the South." There's so much civil rights movement stuff going on down there, I hope the trip won't be too exciting. I don't want any sit-ins or demonstrations while we're there. My parents said we don't have to worry about that. But how do they know? Does all that stuff stop just because it is Christmas and there is supposed to be "peace on earth and good will toward men?" I doubt it.

Thursday, December 19

Nancy and I got into the car for the ride to choir and Mom

started giving instructions to both of us. She announced, "We leave for Knoxville one week from today and we've got to get organized." It's like suddenly she decided we are behind or something.

We drove past the drugstore. "No ice cream today. I packed graham crackers for you. It won't be drippy as you make your lists." Then she dictated what we were to pack. By the time we got to choir, we were thirsty and in foul moods but we both had 10 items on our list. Packing shouldn't be such a big deal. Choir helped. Singing Christmas music always makes me feel better. By the time I got into the car for the ride home, I was over the loss of my ice cream cone, and on the radio, we listened to the Beach Boys singing "Little Saint Nick."

It's amazing what those two crummy pieces of paper did for my mother. Those lists made her happy. Not just happy: *really* happy. She thinks she got something big accomplished. At home, we taped the lists to the refrigerator. Now Mom feels like we are "in control" of the upcoming trip. *Oh, brother.*

Friday, December 20

Christmas vacation! Hooray! School today was a snap because even the teachers were thinking about the break. We just had to get through the day, and we did.

At dinner tonight, Nancy and Mom talked about today's winter holiday program at Temple Israel. Linda went, too. Mom said Rabbi Rubenstein welcomed everyone and said his congregation was pleased to be able to help. She said the Rabbi stayed for the music program and had punch and cookies afterwards. Mom chatted with Rabbi Rubenstein. She said he was very nice. Nancy's string quartet played "Jingle Bells." I've heard it a million times. With a little luck, she'll forget about practicing it and just play it for Nana and Aunt Bette when they come for Christmas.

Margaret and her family leave for Georgia tomorrow. I told her, "I'm going south, too." It's weird. She feels like she is going home, and I feel like I'm going to another country.

Saturday, December 21

This weekend was all about final preparations for Christmas – decorating the tree, wrapping presents, and making cookies. (Mom bakes too many nasty-tasting date nut bars.) Tree decorating is fun, but a hassle. Dad put the tree up. Mom put the lights on. Then, Nancy and I put the ornaments on while Mom directed us. If we got the ornaments on perfectly, there wasn't a lot of switching around. But if we didn't, Mom would swoop in for some serious fine-tuning. We must have a *perfect* tree.

Nancy lost interest in tree trimming before me. Linda wanted to help but she just got in the way. We were patient with her until after the cookie break. While Mom and I were in the kitchen, Linda dragged over the big rocker, climbed up and tossed fistfuls of silver tinsel on the tree. Mom went to see where she was and found her teetering with one foot on the armrest. That's when Mom really yelled. Linda didn't like that, and she started howling. A major repair to our previously *almost perfect* Christmas tree was required. Mom stayed furious for the rest of the afternoon. Linda single-handedly put a damper on the holiday family together time. Nancy and I were in quiet disbelief as we helped Mom re-tinsel the tree.

Sunday, December 22

At church, we sang great Christmas carols. I don't remember anything about the sermon because nothing extraordinary happened this past week in the civil rights movement. They gave us a break.

I love talking with Linda about Santa. I ask questions and Linda rattles off answers about what he's going to do and how he's going to get to our house. I nod and encourage her and inside I am smiling.

Monday, December 23

After she sweetened us up with cinnamon toast, hot chocolate and marshmallows this morning, Mom served up the refrigerator door lists. Nancy and I spent the entire morning with lists in hand, collecting stuff to go into the suitcase we're sharing. Not what we had in mind for the first day of vacation.

I can't wait for tomorrow because Nana is coming home! I've missed her. Nana and Aunt Bette are staying with Linda while we're in Knoxville. Two adults on one kid. It doesn't seem like she's *that* much trouble.

Wednesday, December 25

On Christmas morning Dad goes downstairs to put a fire in the fireplace, put the Christmas music on and set up the movie camera. We don't go down until everyone is dressed, which is easy for Mom, Nancy, Linda, Nana, and me. Not so easy for Aunt Bette. This morning, she took a shower, fussed with her hair and put her make-up on carefully before she even *thought* about going downstairs. Nancy and I danced around, saying, "Come on Aunt Bette, you weren't *that* dirty last night. Take your shower after breakfast," and "Your make-up is perfect!" We even begged her by saying "pleeeease?" It's the same every Christmas morning! When we finally get downstairs, the lights are on and the camera is rolling.

First, Linda checked to see if Santa took the cookies, she left out for him. He did. Mom passed out the stockings and we opened them. At the same time, Dad was shifting back and forth with the camera between the actresses as we opened our stocking presents. Every once in a while, he'd holler, "Hold that up so I can get the picture."

We ate breakfast and returned to the living room for more presents. Once again, Mom passed out the gifts. Some families take turns opening presents, but not ours. Dad's always last, though, because he's the camera man. Sometimes Mom takes pictures of Dad but not today. We were in a hurry.

I love my presents: a new sweater, bookends, bubble bath, lipstick, and a new diary with blank pages! Mom made me a new skirt, blouse and vest. Kakie gave me a pair of long white gloves that stretch way up past my elbows. Her card said, "You are a young lady and soon you'll go to fancy formal dances. You'll need these!" I'm not sure about that. Ahmee and Grandpa always give me a piece of silver. I got a salad fork for my camphor chest. I don't need a salad fork right now.

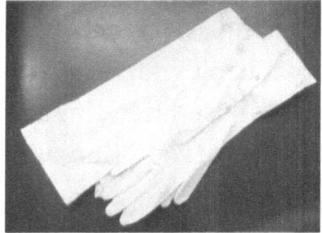

Pretty gloves I'll NEVER use!

After unwrapping and putting away presents, we cleaned up the mess. Mom spent the entire day with her lists. She had lists for Aunt Bette and Nana, so they knew what to do. They listened to her explain, nodded and smiled. Dad hauled all the wedding gifts and luggage out to the station wagon. By 7:00 we had eaten dinner, cleaned the kitchen and packed the car. I was playing cards with Nana and Aunt Bette when Mom said, "Time for bed." I can't sleep yet. I'm too excited about tomorrow's trip.

Thursday, December 26

Wow! What a long day of driving. It is 7:30 p.m. and we're in our Howard Johnson's motel rooms in Roanoke, Virginia. Nancy and I share a room. Mom and Dad are next door. Nancy is watching TV while I am writing. We arrived here just in time. It began snowing when we got to Roanoke, which makes Mom very nervous.

As we drove, I got excited about seeing new places. We went over the George Washington Bridge from New York into New Jersey. We ate turkey sandwiches as we crossed into Pennsylvania. That scenery looked familiar. But in the afternoon, we reached Virginia. When we stopped to gas up and use the restroom, I saw two signs that said: White Women, White Men. I didn't see the signs for Negro travelers.

We saw many small towns with white clapboard houses, wrap-around porches and white picket fences. The houses look so different from the houses back home. There were some boring parts of the day, so Nancy and I played the license plate game and "Twenty Questions." I was glad Mom didn't smoke in the car. Dad asked her not to.

Friday, December 27

Today's drive was shorter, gloomier and mostly depressing. We went through the Smoky Mountains, past miles and miles of trees. It was a little snowy at first but then it changed to gray-brown blah. I saw lots of homes that I wouldn't want to live in, many just cabins or shacks. Some had junk piled up in the front yard – old cars, lumber, and trailers. Everything looked broken. There wouldn't be a house for miles and then we would see an old rusty car off the side of the road. One even had bushes growing out of it. I thought of my train ride to New York City last spring and told myself that it was just a different kind of graffiti.

Shortly after lunch, we arrived at the Knoxville Holiday Inn. Dale and Debbie were waiting for us. Dad's rented tux was also waiting at the motel. We got settled into our rooms. Mom had Dad try his tux on and there was a big problem. Too tight and too short. When Nancy and I saw him squeezed into that pair of pants with his ankles on full display, we started laughing our heads off. Dad snapped, "Don't be DIRKs," which is his abbreviation for "dirty, insolent, rotten kids." That made us laugh even more. He wasn't really mad at us, but he had a problem that needed to be solved right away. Off he went to the tux store.

Later, Uncle Van stopped by with his bride, Marcia, and she is *oh* so pretty. She has a Southern accent very different from Margaret's.

The rehearsal dinner deserves a full report but right now I want to goof around with Debbie. She told me she got a portable record player for Christmas. I'm so jealous! She can play 45s and LPs in her bedroom with her door shut. Dale is 17 now and acts like she is too old for goofing around. Debbie told me Dale has a new boyfriend, Larry, so she's in her own little world.

Saturday, December 28

Wedding day today. Since it's too early to get dressed, I'll write about the rehearsal dinner. It was held at the Cherokee Club, a swanky Knoxville country club. There's a first time for everything, and that was my first time at a country club. *Wow!* The bride's sister, Bonnie, had the job of making sure our family got to where we were supposed to be. At the club, a well-dressed, elderly Negro man opened the front door for us and said, "Good evening, Miss Bonnie. Special day today, isn't it?" He smiled kindly at the rest of us. She smiled back and said, "Yes, it is," but she didn't introduce us. Of course, the only people I knew at the rehearsal dinner were my cousins, their parents and Uncle Van. We were outnumbered by all those Southerners. They all had accents, and it was like they were speaking some foreign language, especially if they talked fast.

The Cherokee Country Club was beautiful. There was a main dining room with a huge side room with a gigantic polished wooden bar. We learned that Marcia's family donated the bar. They're lumber people, so they had it built especially for the club. There was also a beautiful ballroom next to the dining room. More about that later. The dining room was big and fancy – crystal chandelier, white linen tablecloths, flowers and sparkly silver. Bonnie said the windows overlooked the Tennessee River, but it was too dark to see. The adults had drinks before dinner. We kids had ginger ale and hors d'oeuvres galore. I ate a ton of cashews. Nancy went for the shrimp. Dinner was formal and not what I am used to. There were so many forks; Mom told us which fork to use for which course.

We were served dinner by older Negro gentlemen dressed in white dinner jackets which reminded me of Dad's tux. They even wore short white gloves. There were so many waiters ready, willing and able to serve us. They stood back from the table and watched until they noticed a need and then, boom! It was taken care of in no time. Whenever one of the waiters talked to Nancy or me, he called us "Miss." No one ever called me that before, unless it was Mom and she was mad at me.

After our crème brule dessert and toasts to the bride and groom, there was more adult small talk. I asked to be excused to go to the bathroom. On my way back, I saw a party in the ballroom. I hurried to ask Mom if I could look and she said, "Yes, it's a debutante ball." I stood behind a big column at the side of the ballroom and watched a pageant, a parade that reminded me of *Gone with the Wind*. The ballroom was filled with people dressed to the nines. The women were in elegant, long dresses. The men wore tuxedos. Before this trip, I'd only seen tuxedos in movies on TV. By the time we get home, I probably will have seen about a hundred tuxedos including Dad's. Round tables with Christmassy centerpieces were at both sides of the room. The staircase and center aisle led to a dance floor. The band was off to the side.

As the band played, a grown-up girl entered at the top of the ballroom stairs. Her dad met her in the middle of the landing. Then someone announced on the microphone, "Presenting Miss Christine Jackson Tollefson." At that point, the beaming father escorted his beautiful daughter down the red carpeted stairs to the front of the ballroom. The seated guests clapped, and flash bulbs went off non-stop. The girls stood together in a single line, waiting for the others. After everyone had been presented, the band played a song for the dads' and daughters' first dance.

The debutante girls weren't much older than me, maybe 17 or 18. They were beautiful in their floor-length white gowns. They carried pink bouquets. Every girl wore long white gloves, just like my new gloves. They looked like brides or princesses. Everyone was smiling. The dads' smiles were mixed with pride, pride, pride. I wondered about the moms. They sat at the tables smiling with the others, but they certainly weren't center stage. It was all about the girls and their dads. Standing along the walls, I saw a lot of Negro men, all dressed up in bow ties, dinner jackets, and with those white gloves, just waiting to serve the white folks.

Sunday, December 29

We're on our way home. If the weather behaves there will be some interesting stops along the way. Jamestown, Williamsburg and Washington, D.C. Now for the wedding wrap-up.

Yesterday was cold with a bit of snow on the ground. The bride and groom got married at the Second Presbyterian Church in West Knoxville. They each had three attendants. The bridesmaids wore long green velvet dresses and carried white flowers.

The wedding went off as planned and when they walked out of the church, I heard Marcia turn to Uncle Van and say, "We're hitched!" The reception was held in the church hall. Lots of hugs, kisses, punch, nuts, mints and, of course, wedding cake. After the reception, the family went back to Marcia's home for another party and, we thought, dinner. Marcia's home reminded me of Brooke's house without a butler or a cook. Her house is a three-story red brick with dark brown trim. We walked into the foyer and saw the living room on the right. It had beautiful built-in bookcases next to the fireplace. The wood was probably from their family lumber business. In one living room corner, there was a baby grand piano and the look I got from Mom shouted, "Don't even think about touching that piano." The bride and groom made a telephone call to Ahmee and Grandpa Ray. I'm not sure why my grandparents missed this special day.

At the church, our mothers told us not to eat too many sweets because we would spoil our appetites for dinner. We had eaten brunch, so we were only running on one meal. We couldn't wait for dinner. We were starving. The party talky-talk just kept going on and on, and dinner was never served. When Debbie and I asked our mothers, they shushed us and told us we'd eat when we got back to the motel. But when we got there, the restaurant was closed. Dad bought us a bunch of candy bars from the vending machine. So much for not eating sweets before dinner.

Monday, December 30

We are home. We are tired. Yesterday we drove hard and kept changing our plans all day because a storm was coming. Mom gets so nervous when we drive in bad weather, especially if it is snowing. We left Knoxville at 5:30 a.m. After breakfast, we made a quick stop at a plantation. It really was a run-through instead of a walk-through, but at least I saw a plantation. I thought plantations were white and huge like Tara. This *red brick* plantation was much smaller than I expected. We saw the shacks where slaves had lived. One beautiful home and then just steps away was a home that's best described as a hovel.

Later we took the ferry to Jamestown and made an even shorter stop there. It was windy and freezing cold. Mom didn't even get out of the car except to smoke, and I was wishing I didn't have to. We didn't stop at Williamsburg. It was, "See the old buildings and the old styles? Can't get out because that storm is coming." In the cloudy afternoon, we drove through Washington, D.C. It was depressing to see all the flags at half-staff to honor President Kennedy. And it was even sadder to see the black drapes framing the North Portico door of the White House.

I was glad to get home. When we arrived, Aunt Bette and Nana were packed and ready to go. The snow was just starting to come down. I hope they make it okay.

Tuesday, December 31

We are snowed in. Who cares? Mom's happy after yesterday's long day of worrying. Nana called to say they made it without any trouble. So, let it snow, snow, snow. It's New Year's Eve, but we'll turn in as usual.

My diary is filled up. I'll start the new one tomorrow, which seems appropriate.

A snowy day on Merry Lane.

Postscript from Carol-Anne
2020

I loved seeing the Debutante Ball but at the same time, it was very confusing to me. Four months earlier the March on Washington for Jobs and Freedom had taken place. Many, many people – black and white – marched for freedom for black Americans; I knew some of the marchers. I understood that black people wanted jobs – good jobs and they wanted freedom which meant, at the very least, access to public drinking fountains and restrooms, access to good teachers and education, full participation in elections, and the chance to live where they wanted to live.

The Debutante Ball seemed like a step back from the March on Washington. All the guests were white. The young girls and women wore beautiful long gowns and long white gloves just like the ones I got for Christmas.

There were lots of black waiters dressed in fancy uniforms wearing white gloves. Was that the job – waiting on white people at a country club event – the "good job, the decent job" that people marched for in August? I didn't think so because the Debutante Ball was mostly white people sitting around, eating, dancing, enjoying themselves and black waiters doing everything they could to make it a great evening for those guests.

What do you think?

1964

Here and There News
January 1964

Wednesday, January 1, 1964!

Brand new year! Brand new diary! Even brand-new snow. It's a winter wonderland outside. We're sledding this morning and watching the Rose Bowl Parade later. Dad has dibs on the TV this afternoon because he's watching the Rose Bowl Game. I am rooting for Illinois because it's closer to us than the state of Washington. That's about as dumb a reason as any, but I don't like to watch football and not root for somebody. It's weird to think of Ahmee and Grandpa Ray sitting out in sunny California, watching the same parade and football game but without any snow.

Mom suggested I start on my thank-you notes. Thanks, but no thanks, Mom. I can't face them yet.

Friday, January 3

This new diary doesn't lie as flat as my old one. It's stiff but I love the blank pages. Now I can write if I want and not worry about writing into the next day's space. It's freer.

Dad barked at me today when I said, "I think I should be able to wear slacks to GFS." He said, "You are too young to know what you think." Does he *really believe* that or is it the way to totally stop the conversation and make me go away? I might not be talking then, but I am still thinking. In a diary, no one can say, "You can't write about that." It's quiet around here except for Nancy's practicing. She has been sawing away to catch up on her missed violin practice times. Linda was glad to have us home. She's been following Mom around like a shadow.

Sunday, January 5

Back to the old routines now. Church, choir and Sunday school. I don't think about BZ Boy #1 ever, and that's a relief.

Margaret called this afternoon. My parents let me have a 20-minute catch-up conversation. We talked about our Christmas travels. It wasn't private though, because the kitchen phone is right in the center of everything. Nancy was practicing in the living room and the sound came through the kitchen wall. The TV was on, too. I wish my parents would let me use the telephone in their room. Anyway, I told Margaret about the wedding and the debutante ball. She was jealous that I got to see the debs. I joked that none of those girls had bells on their dresses. Her reply? "Oh, you just had to chime in about that. Don't remind me, you ding-a-ling!"

Monday, January 6

Back to school today. With Margaret around, it's so much more bearable. We find plenty to talk about, even though we were on the phone yesterday.

My favorite magazine came and Dr. Martin Luther King Jr. was on the cover as *Time* "Man of the Year." It's great because he was everywhere, preaching nonviolence and hope for a better future for Negroes. The article said that 1963 was the "centennial of the Emancipation Proclamation." I didn't know that. I said something about it to Mom, and Nancy asked, "What's that?" Mom said, "It's the hundredth anniversary of when slaves were freed." Somehow it makes the civil rights movement so much more necessary and important. Why does it take 100 years to get rights in this country?

Time mentioned everything that happened this past year: the Children's Crusade, the Birmingham bombings, and the March on Washington. They forgot the murder of Medgar Evers. *Time* said Dr. King is the "symbol of that revolution." If it *is* a revolution, I'd rather have Dr. King's nonviolent revolution instead of a revolution with guns.

Martin Luther King Jr. is 5 feet 7 inches tall. I am as tall as he is! If we ever met, we'd probably see about eye to eye. He gets up at 6:30 a.m. and reads. He drinks fruit juice, has coffee and goes to his office. He eats lunch at his desk. Sometimes he doesn't go home until two or three o'clock in the morning. I bet his kids really miss him when he works those long days.

My favorite sentence from the article is, "he has stirred in his people a Christian forbearance that nourishes hope and smothers injustice." I don't know why that sentence says so much to me. I am a white Christian girl who doesn't have the same kind of experiences that Negro people have, but life should be fairer for everyone. And without hope, what is there?

Wednesday, January 8

Girl Scouts today and Margaret and I are plodding through the First Class Scout requirements.

There's an article about the new President and his wife, Lady Bird Johnson, in *Time* magazine. (What a name, "Lady

Bird.") They seem like nice people. Then there was a story about "Three Widows." It was sad because it was about Mrs. Kennedy's and Mrs. Tippett's family Christmas. Mrs. Tippett's husband was killed in Dallas the day President Kennedy died. It was also about Mrs. Oswald, who said this was her best Christmas ever because her husband was "difficult." Many people sent money and presents for her children because they felt sorry for them.

Thursday, January 9

When we were at the drug store today, so was Glenda, the shoplifter. I saw her on my way out the door. We were in a hurry to get to choir, so I couldn't see what she was up to. I don't know what I would do if I saw her take something.

Friday, January 10

It would have been better if we hadn't had ballroom dancing tonight. That weirdo Billy Beboe kept smirking and saying, "What, no bells tonight?" Margaret doesn't care as much as I do. She had a quick, smart aleck response that almost shut him up. I just want to forget the whole thing.

Sunday, January 12

Saturday, on the 6:00 news, there was a story about the dangers of smoking. I was watching, but Mom called us for dinner, so I had to turn the TV off and miss most of it. Yesterday's newspaper reported that smoking kills people. I immediately started to worry about Mom, Nana and Aunt Bette because they all smoke. Dad smokes his pipe or sometimes a disgusting cigar. But he doesn't smoke every day like Mom does. I don't want Mom to die. So, I decided to talk with her about the hazards of smoking and how I want her to quit.

After we ate Sunday supper, we had the 6:00 news on. Mom was cleaning up the kitchen. When the story about smoking cigarettes came on, I told her to come watch. Right then, she had a cigarette in the ashtray on the kitchen counter. We watched the news together and then I told her that if she quit smoking, I never would start. She looked at me very seriously.

"What?" she asked.

I said, "Mom, if you quit smoking, I promise I'll never smoke."

"Never?"

And I said, "Never, I promise."

Mom picked up the cigarette in the ashtray and stamped it out. Maybe she had already been thinking about quitting but making that promise to her about me not smoking really worked. Now we must get her through these next few days and weeks because the TV guys said it's hard. I hope I can convince Nana and Aunt Bette, too, but first we must get Mom over the hump.

Tuesday, January 14

Well, I am feeling very smart because in social studies, we had to choose a current event topic and write a report. When Mr. Nelson asked, "What current event do you choose?" my hand shot up. "The March on Washington!" Mr. Nelson said it was a very good idea. Those notes and the *Time* magazines that I have saved from last August will really come in handy.

Mom isn't smoking, and she isn't very happy. I am, though.

Saturday, January 18

On the news tonight, they showed pictures of President Johnson and Dr. King meeting. The new President looks exhausted and Dr. King looks very serious, very determined. I can guess what they were talking about, and there aren't any easy answers since there are so many people who don't care about equal rights for everyone.

Why is speaking up for equal rights so hard for people? Maybe because if you have the rights you need you might not care about the rights of other people. Or maybe you'd be nervous and think that if someone gets more rights, you might lose some of your own... and in that case, it's probably easier not to do anything.

Thursday, January 23

Nancy's 10 today. She is acting like she's a teenager. *She's not.* Presents, cake, and ice cream. That's the birthday routine here on Merry Lane.

Something unusual happened today. Our country got the 24th Amendment to the Constitution. This will be the topic of conversation in social studies tomorrow. I'm ready because I know that this amendment outlaws the use of poll taxes in national elections, which means states can't charge people to vote. That's a good idea because some people might have the money to pay and others might not.

I've got to work on my social studies report. The outline is due on Monday.

Saturday, January 25

I haven't been too enthusiastic about writing lately but I feel like my mood is going to change.

The Winter Olympics start soon. Nana and I like to watch the skaters on TV in her bedroom. The newspaper listed the skaters, and I found one from Great Britain who has the same name as me, almost. Carol-Ann Warner. She even has a *hyphen!* No question about it: I'll root for Carol-Ann and Peggy Fleming.

Pancakes for dinner tonight. Why do we have to have breakfast for dinner? What's that all about, anyway? These days Mom is mostly eating cheese slice after cheese slice.

Nothing on TV tonight so I'm in my room, door closed, comfy cozy in my four-poster bed, writing. I've got my transistor radio on and I'm listening to Murray the K, my favorite deejay. He is on WINS, and he plays the most terrific songs and says, "What's happening, baby?" All the kids at school say that, too. Everyone listens to Murray the K.

I love when he plays the Beach Boys, the Four Seasons and Dionne Warwick. On Thursday night, he talked about some new group from England. I don't remember their name.

Margaret Chase Smith for President?

Monday, January 27

Amazing news keeps happening. Today Senator Margaret Chase Smith announced she's running for President of the United States. She hasn't got a chance, but she is going to give it a try. She's a Republican just like Ahmee and Grandpa, but I bet they'll be pulling for a man – maybe Barry Goldwater.

It's been two weeks now since Mom quit smoking. She's grouchy, and according to the newspaper, that's to be expected. She eats Muenster and Swiss cheese when she wants a cigarette and that seems to help. Since I don't like cheese, quitting smoking would be twice as hard for me. I'll never start.

Tuesday, January 28

Last night, I got into bed and listened to the radio. The new fantastic singing group is named the Beatles. I love their songs "I Want to Hold Your Hand" and "She Loves You." All the girls were talking about their favorite Beatle, but I couldn't picture any of them.

I bet anything before too long "I Want to Hold Your Hand" will be #1 on the charts. All the girls were singing it at the top of their lungs on the bus home today. Last week the Beatles album, *Meet the Beatles*, was released. Frances already has it. She is feeling proud of herself since she is English just like John, Paul, George and Ringo. Some of the girls at school were saying the album is sold out in Westport and Norwalk. Lucky for me Frances already got her copy. I can listen to it at her house.

Margaret said the Beatles were going to be on *The Ed Sullivan Show* in February. I will be right there, eyes glued to the TV, watching. I hope Dad doesn't get the idea that I don't need to watch TV that night.

Postscript from Carol-Anne
2020

In 1963, I watched the Evening News *and read* Time *magazine and became more interested in the civil rights movement, the famous people who were a part of the movement and especially Martin Luther King Jr. They were the people who believed in an idea and tried to encourage change for the better by doing something!*

I knew one person who was trying to nurture change to make the world a better place and that was Miss Simpson, my GFS leader. On Saturday mornings, she talked with me about important issues and made things happen. She attended the March on Washington. She put together the sleepover with the girls from New York City. She put words into action. She was one person who made a difference in my life.

I didn't know Margaret Chase Smith, but I respected her from a distance. She was a United States Senator who took action when she announced she was a candidate for President of the United States. She was a role model for other women. She inspired other women to believe that they too could be a state representative, senator or even president.

In college my professor, Mr. Nelson, told me "You have good ideas. Take that idea and run with it." That comment has lasted me a lifetime! If it is a good idea put it to good use. There is a chance that idea might influence someone, somewhere and something positive might happen.

I've watched and learned from those teachers and many others. Miss Simpson and Margaret Chase Smith encouraged me and showed me – by their actions – to think new ideas. Teachers encourage and help. Some of my teachers taught me that thinking about ideas and doing something with those ideas could be important work.

I remember that I was one of my sister's first teachers because I taught her to read. I encouraged my mom to quit smoking. I think those early life experiences inspired me to become a teacher.

Who has encouraged you? Have you ever encouraged someone else? Are you involved in anything today that might be a hint as to what the future holds for you?

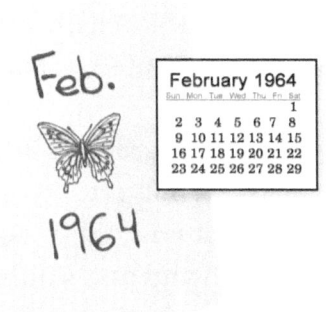

February Ups and Downs
February 1964

Tuesday, February 4

I took a few days off from writing. I got busy doing absolutely nothing. We had the Olympics on whenever we could.

Over the weekend, I wrote a six-page letter to Judy. It went on and on, like hers do, about school and church stuff plus the Beatles and Senator Margaret Chase Smith. I told Judy I was confused about Mrs. Smith. She seems nice and smart, so I don't understand why she would throw her name into the presidential ring when there is *no chance* she'll get nominated. Seems like a lot of trouble for no results. I guess she's thinking there ought to be one woman who will be first, and at least give it a try. Judy will probably sit right down and write a response. I wish she'd calm down and write two weeks from now, so I don't have to worry about writing her again before next weekend.

Only nine more days until Mom is at a month of no smoking. Our house doesn't smell smoky like it used to.

Friday, February 7

Yippee! I got an A on my March on Washington social studies report! Mr. Nelson commented, "This report is complete and well written!"

Dance class tonight. Margaret and I dread this routine. We like the ride over and back but putting up with the immature boys there is painful. Right now, there's only one person I would want to dance with and that's only because he is taller than me. His name is Don. Who knows if he is nice? He is so quiet. Margaret has her eye on Art because he laughs at her jokes.

Saturday, February 8

Nana and I watched the figure skaters today. It is amazing to see them spin, twirl and jump. When I'm on the ice, I hold my breath and pray I don't fall. Olympic skaters make it look so easy. I'm jealous.

Sunday, February 9

We had a terrible drive to church today. It was beginning to snow as we drove up the hill and it looked like ice. Mom suggested we go home. Dad said, "No, we can make it. We'll be fine." Well, we didn't make it. As we started down the hill to Cannondale, the car skidded and went sideways until we landed in a ditch. Nancy's nose was in her book when we hit the ice. She perked up when Mom started screaming. My eyes were about ready to pop, and Dad never said a word, but he was biting the inside of his mouth. He was scared just like the rest of us because of that pond at the bottom of the hill. After the car stopped, Mom sobbed, and we were quiet. Then she said, "I need a cigarette."

Dad shook his head, "Bobbie, you've made it so far. Don't

start up now. Let's go home." We got out of the car and with help from people who live at the bottom of the hill, Dad pushed the car out of the ditch. Mom, Nancy, Linda and I stood out of the way and watched. My feet were freezing because I got snow in my slip-ons. The quiet drive home took forever. No church for the Hughes family today.

On a happier note, the Beatles are on *The Ed Sullivan Show* in four hours. Yesterday, Dad said there was no good reason to watch *The Ed Sullivan Show* tonight. He sounded serious. I found a quiet moment with Mom to get her to promise that I can watch the Beatles. Mom didn't think it was a big deal, but I told her I don't want to be the only kid in town who doesn't watch. She told me to finish my homework and be all ready for Monday morning, so I'm doing that next.

Monday, February 10

The Beatles were unbelievable! *WOW!* The girls in the audience were going absolutely crazy and, honestly, I would have too, if I'd been there. The TV had some close-up shots. Paul is my favorite. At the beginning of the show, they sang "All My Loving," "Till There Was You" and "She Loves You." One funny part was when they showed John's face, there was a caption that said, "Sorry girls, he's married." At the end of the show, the Beatles performed again. This time they sang "I Saw Her Standing There" and "I Want to Hold Your Hand." Two months ago, nobody even knew who they were.

At school, all the girls talked about the Beatles. They were singing or humming Beatle songs. Some argued about the lyrics because the British accents were hard to understand. Frances usually chimed in and got the last word. Everyone was telling everyone else who she thought was the cutest Beatle, the smartest Beatle, and the funniest Beatle. There was no end to the Beatles discussions. One girl from school,

Trisha, is acting so stuck up and like she's so special. She's got the Beatles bubble gum cards and said if the Beatles ever gave a concert in New York, she would go, no matter where it was. She's already discussed this with her mom who said it would be okay. She's just waiting for the concert to be announced. I would never mention this to my parents because I know the answer would be "no."

Next Sunday the Beatles are going to be on *The Ed Sullivan Show* again. It's unusual but I'm not complaining.

Tuesday, February 11

This week's *Time* magazine is all bad news. Cold War. South Vietnam. The Congo: Massacre Season. Public Schools: New York Dilemma. Civil Rights: Ruining a Reputation. It's a mess everywhere in the U.S. and the world. I flipped through to find something easier to deal with and I did. There's an article about Margaret Chase Smith. She's served three terms in the Senate. She's set a Senate roll call record because she was there for 1,590 successive votes. Talk about perfect attendance! She shows up a lot!

The "People" section says the Swedish Parliament nominated Martin Luther King Jr. for the 1964 Nobel Peace Prize. It says the nomination was made because of Dr. King's nonviolent efforts for civil rights. It's no surprise they didn't nominate Bull Connor or George Wallace.

Wednesday, February 12

I love February because we always get Abraham Lincoln's birthday off and George Washington's, too.

It looks like it might snow. Better snow than ice. I'm hoping for cold, cold weather and no snow. If that happens, then Janice will invite me over to ice skate like she did last year. She lives in an old house on Olmstead Hill Road. Her house is about 100 years old. It has a huge fireplace in the kitchen that is always going in the wintertime. Their pond is nestled down in the woods and sometimes you can hear a little echo. Last year, we were the only one's skating. Janice can skate backwards and twirl around a little bit. I just try to skate forward and not fall. After skating, Janice's mom made hot chocolate for us. If I think about it, I can still taste it.

Sunday, February 16

I haven't written because I had an accident with my finger on Valentine's Day. Accidents shouldn't happen around birthdays or other special days. Last Thursday, as predicted, an ice storm hit. Sleet was coming down as the bus dropped us off. It was slippery underfoot but Nancy, Frances and I made it down the hill. Of course, that horrible Mrs. Oots picked up her girls but didn't offer us a ride. Mom didn't pick us up because she was concentrating on a sewing project.

As Nancy and I walked up the driveway, Mom knocked on the dining room window and pointed at the mailbox. I turned to go back and slipped on a sheet of black ice. I came down hard on my left hand. My ring finger started to swell before I got to the house. I was crying because it really hurt. Fortunately, Nana was home, so she watched my sisters while Mom and I made the drive to Wilton. Driving was awful because the roads were so slick. On the way down the hill to Cannondale, we were fishtailing all over the place. At one point, Mom and I were both in tears.

At the doctor's office, the first thing he did was cut my signet ring off and take X-rays of my finger. He put a splint on and sent us home. He told Mom to call in the morning for the X-ray results. We stopped at the train station, waited for Dad, and he drove the rest of the way. At home, I got into Nana's bed, had a good cry and watched TV until I fell asleep.

I woke up when the TV station was signing off for the day with "Taps" and the fuzzy snow that shows all night until the National Anthem kicks in the next morning.

On Friday morning, it was off to another doctor's office in Westport. His name? Dr. Hughes, same as our last name. More X-rays, which showed I didn't break my finger. I *crushed* my knuckle. He said my finger was "smashed to smithereens." No problem though, he could fix it by putting a pin all the way through the end of my finger. In one side and out the other. He added a rubber band to each side, looped them over two pieces of coat hanger wire and pulled the end of my finger straight. He finished off his work with a full hand cast. When the procedure was over, he was all smiles. I was fighting to hold back more tears. Who wants a pin sticking out both sides of her finger? Mom told me that Dr. Hughes was a doctor for the Olympic team. Who cares? He stuck a pin through me. When Nana saw, she was so sympathetic and said, "Oh, Carolee, that's awful. I'll get you a present next time I'm out!"

Now I have a really gross-looking finger. The pin stays in for at least six weeks. I can't get any kind of mitten or glove on, so I have to wrap my whole hand. I'm using that pink scarf George gave me in fourth grade. It looks okay but it doesn't keep my hand warm in this weather. A couple of times I have gotten the pin caught on a sweater or my coat and the pain bring tears to my eyes. Sleeping is no easy matter because I have to balance my hand just right to be sure it doesn't get caught on anything. It's miserable.

I watched the Beatles on *The Ed Sullivan Show* tonight in Nana's room, so Dad didn't have to listen. Thank goodness we have two TVs. Tonight, they sang "She Loves You," "This Boy," "All My Loving," "I Saw Her Standing There" and "I Want to Hold Your Hand." The cameras showed way too much of the screaming girls. I just wanted to see Paul and the other guys.

I dread going to school tomorrow with my finger and the

pin sticking out of it. And another thing: how is Dr. Hughes going to get this out?

Monday, February 17

At school today when I should have been in PE class, I was holding court in the school library. Even kids I didn't know wanted to see the pin through the end of my finger. Everyone agreed it's repulsive. One kid asked, "How do you stand it?" I didn't have a choice. One good thing: I have an excused absence from PE for the next six weeks. The bad part is that for the first time, Margaret is mad at me...well, sort of. She's just jealous because I don't have to go.

Transistor Radio is Fun, Fun, Fun!

My radio is on and I just heard the Beach Boys sing "Fun, Fun, Fun." I love that song, but I am not having fun, fun, fun with this pin in my finger.

Friday, February 21

No school today, so I am reading *To Kill a Mockingbird*. Now I know why Judy was after me to read it last summer. I can't put it down. It takes place in a small southern town. In the story, Mr. Raymond talks to one of the children, Dill, about "the hell white people give colored folks, without even stopping to think that they're people, too." That sentence reminds me of life today.

Saturday, February 22

At GFS this morning, all the girls wanted to see my finger. They looked, even though it just grossed them all out. Nobody else in the family wants to look at my hand either.

I finished *To Kill a Mockingbird*. Judy is right. It *is* first-rate. The story is told by Scout, a not too lady-like young girl who reports about life on her street and in her small hometown. It's a sad story about a Negro man who is unfairly accused of raping a white woman.

One scary part of the book reminded me of times when I've walked home from Frances' house at the end of the day when it's getting dark. Nobody's following me but it feels as if someone is in the woods and my heart really gets thumping. In the story, when Bob Ewell follows Scout and her brother home after dark, my heart was really pounding. In another part of the story, Scout's dad, Atticus, tells his children, "In our courts when it's a white man's word against a black man's, the white man always wins. They're ugly but those are the facts of life." So sad and not the way it's supposed to be in our country. I hope it's not always this way.

Sunday, February 23

The Beatles were on *Ed Sullivan* again tonight. I bet this will be the last time. Tonight, they sang "Twist and Shout," "Please, Please Me" and "I Want to Hold Your Hand." Nana and Mom watched with me. Dad was nowhere to be seen.

Monday, February 24

I'm catching up on *Time* magazines. Today I read that Mrs. Marina Oswald believes her husband killed President Kennedy because he wanted to be popular. Almost everyone wants to be popular. He'll be well-known, but not for good reasons.

Margaret and I have decided to have a more mature, positive attitude at next week's dance class. I'm not certain how this will work but we'll try. Dancing's going to be awkward with my finger.

Wednesday, February 26

In the library during PE time, I found the January edition of *Look* magazine and there's a painting by Norman Rockwell. It's about Ruby Bridges, the little Negro girl who went to school by herself because the parents of the other first graders took their kids out of school. All those kids were white. In the picture, Ruby is escorted by federal marshals as she goes into school. She looks so cute, all dressed up with a white bow in her hair, carrying a couple of books and a ruler. On the wall next to her is the splat of a tomato and "n----r," so it's obvious what it's supposed to mean. And to think she was just a little girl going to school.

I must study for the science test tomorrow.

Thursday, February 27

I usually don't get into trouble at school, but I did today, and Margaret was right there with me.

We had a science test and Mr. Joldersma, one of the regular subs, was there today because Mrs. Kragthorpe is out for two weeks. Some kids were giving him trouble, but Margaret and I were behaving. Just before the test, Margaret reached into her purse to get a pencil. No luck. So, she asked me for one and I tossed an extra to her. Unfortunately, the pencil hit the edge of the desk and bounced forward. Mr. Joldersma yelled, "Who threw that pencil?" I raised my hand thinking, "I didn't throw it. I tossed it."

He said, "Get up here," and immediately wrote out a behavior slip to the principal's office. He said, "You've just failed the test and you have detention for two weeks. Throwing a pencil is very dangerous. You can poke someone's eye out." He didn't give me a chance to explain. Margaret looked sick as I walked out of the room. I don't want to fail the test. I don't deserve detention. It's not fair.

Friday, February 28

I could take the science test today. Even after Mom called the school to complain, I have four days of detention in my science classroom instead of regular detention hall. That's the compromise. Why is it that some people don't understand about what's fair? Some kids in class were really mouthing off. I was trying to help a friend. Our real teacher, Mrs. Kragthorpe, wouldn't have given me detention for that. She understands about fair and unfair. It was easier for the sub to yell at me and send me to the principal's office than it was for him to get the other kids to behave. That's not fair.

BREAKING NEWS
King to Speak at Freedom Rally!

Saturday, February 29

It's Leap Year Day today so it's Miss Simpson's real birthday. She brought her own birthday cake with seven candles. We sang "Happy Birthday" to her and told her she's the youngest GFSer. We all got such a laugh.

Last Thursday, the *Weston Town Crier*, our local paper, had an article about Martin Luther King Jr. He's speaking at a Freedom Rally on March 11 in Bridgeport. That's so close, just about a half hour drive from here. The money they raise at the rally will pay for bail bonds in Georgia and Alabama. I wish I could hear him speak.

Postscript from Carol-Anne
2020

I can't think about my middle school years and not remember Martin Luther King Jr. and all the times he fought for equality and justice for all people. He showed up. He was all over the place – all over our country talking to black and white leaders. Showing up during tough times. That's what he did because he dreamed of a life for his children and all children that was fair. During that time our country needed lots of people to show up – black, brown and white, people of every race. It seemed that Jewish people always showed up and they were the first white people to do so. It took the white Christians a little longer to figure out what to do but many did. I'm not sure about when or if folks from other religions showed up but I guess some of them probably did because in the end, we all need each other. Showing up is so important.

Showing up is doing something. Sometimes, just showing up is doing a lot.

If I had had a different point of view in 1963, I would not just witness the civil rights movement; I would be a part of it. I would not just be a quiet observer. But what could I do? I would talk with my friends about civil rights issues. I would write letters to my state representatives and my local newspaper. Maybe I could even figure out a way to take action to support the Children's Crusade kids who walked out of school to protest unjust laws in Birmingham Alabama.

Now I know that sometimes when I show up for someone or a cause I care about, it's as good for me as it is for the person, I am there for. Have you ever shown up to for someone? Why did you?

Do you think we still need people to show up for civil rights today?

Considerations: Shoplifters and MLK
March 1964

Monday, March 2

Another day of detention and it isn't fun. Mr. Joldersma wouldn't let me do my homework. I had to sit and do nothing until the late bus home. What a waste of time. All the girls who stayed after school for fun activities were singing Beatles songs, but not me.

Wednesday, March 4

Finally, detention's done. Mr. Joldersma saved the best for last because today he made me, and another kid watch him dissect a frog. He said, "It'll be good for you. Tomorrow, you'll be ahead of the rest of the class." He is creepy. I wish I'd kept my hand down when he asked who threw the pencil. I'll be happy when Mrs. Kragthorpe returns.

Thursday, March 5

I had a sore throat when I woke up this morning, so I stayed home and watched TV all day. On *I've Got a Secret*, there was a fireman from Georgetown, which is just down Route 57. It was hysterical because his secret was that he and the other Georgetown firemen were playing cards while the firehouse was on fire. The panelists didn't guess his secret. It was too ridiculous.

Friday, March 6

Poor Margaret! When I caught up with her after her PE class today, she was in tears. She was *really* mad at her mom. Yesterday Mrs. Vernon went shopping and bought Margaret some pettipants, those fancy shorts-like underwear with lace that girls wear instead of a slip. Margaret's mom told her, "The nice thing about pettipants is you don't have to wear underpants." Being the *good* daughter that she is, Margaret believed her mom and went to school. Then in PE, Margaret had to change into her gym shorts. The pettipants hung down 3 inches below the shorts. It was coed gym week and basketball to boot. Margaret said, "I couldn't go to PE without underwear and have coed basketball. So, I rolled up the pettipants as best I could. Every time they slipped down, I would stop and roll them back up again. The boys kept laughing at me and saying, "What's that?" She was humiliated. I bet she gave it to her mother after school.

No dance class for me tonight. I persuaded Mom so I don't have to go. Today at school a kid walked past my desk in math class and brushed against the pin in my finger, it's still throbbing. Poor Margaret is on her own.

Monday, March 9

Time today had an article about the first hundred days of LBJ's presidency. I can't believe he has been president that long. I bet the Kennedy family feels like it's been a lifetime.

My finger *got caught* on my sweater today. It was the worst. I can't wait to be done with this, but how will Dr. Hughes get the pin out? I don't want to think about it.

Thursday, March 12

Today while we were getting ice cream cones at the drugstore, Rita and Glenda were there. Rita was eyeing the candy, especially the Baby Ruths and the red licorice. I wish I could have stayed long enough to see if she took something, but Mom kept saying, "Hurry up! You'll be late for choir."

Saturday, March 14

Not much going on and that's fine with me. It is great to have quiet time. It's a wonderful Saturday afternoon, and everyone is just doing what they want. Mom is sewing, Dad is talking on his ham radio, Nancy is reading, and Nana is keeping Linda amused playing with Linda's dollies. I am in my room, door shut, radio on, writing and wasting the day away. It's the best.

I predict that the March 23 edition of *Time* will have a big article about Jack Ruby and Lee Harvey Oswald's murder. The jury found Ruby guilty of killing Oswald. How could they not? Everyone with a TV saw him do it.

Sunday, March 15

I don't know who Malcolm X is, but he is getting a lot of press these days. There's another interesting name. Glad it isn't mine.

I am reminding myself of Nancy because I am buried in *To Kill a Mockingbird* again.

BREAKING NEWS
King to Speak at Temple Israel in May!

Wednesday, March 18

Most of the time our local paper is about the folks who go on vacations and other boring stuff. Today is different. I found something *really* interesting. Dr. Martin Luther King Jr. is speaking at Temple Israel in Westport on Friday, May 22. That's where Nancy goes to school. Oh gosh, I wish I was a member of that congregation so I could hear him speak. Ever since Dr. King gave his "I Have a Dream" speech last August, I've been fascinated by everything he is trying to do. The newspapers and TV make all his work seem very important, even history-making.

If he wasn't for nonviolence, we could be in a horrible revolution and so many more people would be hurt or even dead. He keeps preaching fairness, justice and equality. He's trying to make our country a better place for Negro people. Actually, he'll make the U.S. a better country for us all.

Thursday, March 19

Rita and Glenda were at the drugstore today. As we waited for our ice cream cones, I saw Rita mosey on over to the candy section. There she was, eyeing all the goodies with her large orange hoop purse just dangling on her wrist. Every so often, she glanced around. Then I noticed Glenda talking to the cashier. She was being oh so very chatty and oh so charming as she paid for her one box of Boston Baked Beans. Meanwhile Rita just brushed a couple of candy bars from the glass shelf into her purse. A couple of seconds later, she brushed a Mr. Goodbar onto the floor and leaned over to pick it up. Isn't she nice? She put it back on the shelf but whoops! Some Milk Duds, Fireballs and Necco Wafers just jumped into her big orange bag. She stepped back from the shelf and selected one package each of Chuckles, Chicklets and Chocolate Candy Cigarettes. She paid for those while Glenda waited, and then the girls walked out of the drugstore together, cool as clams. They had lots to talk about once they were on their way.

When we got in the car, Mom was mad because she wanted to get going. She didn't know why I was dawdling. She had forgotten about this shoplifting stuff. Then when I told her, she was angry with me for not telling on the girls. I don't think I could. Neither Rita nor Glenda are my friends, but I don't want them saying I am a tattletale. Lots of kids think that Rita and Glenda are wonderful because they hand out candy at school all the time. I don't want to make a bunch of enemies.

Friday, March 20

Shoplifting update. Yes, Glenda and Rita were at school today with their private candy store. They both seemed stuck up, smiling and passing out candy right and left in the hallway.

I told Margaret what I'd seen, and she said she wasn't surprised. We agreed we could never shoplift even for "just candy." Stealing is always stealing. We wouldn't fink on them. When I write to Judy, I'm going to ask her if she'd tell. Mom's always telling Linda, "Don't be a tattletale," when Linda tells on me or Nancy about something.

Saturday, March 21

Aunt Bette came from New York City for the weekend. Mom made tacos for lunch. In the afternoon, Frances brought over her Beatles album. We put it on the phonograph in the living room, and Aunt Bette listened with us. She liked some of the songs. Frances and I were singing and dancing like crazy but we had to be careful so the needle wouldn't skip and ruin the record. Mom was sewing and she didn't seem to mind listening to the Beatles.

Dad kept yelling, "Turn it down." Poor Dad.

Monday, March 23

On the way home from school, all the kids were singing Beatles and Beach Boys songs. It was great, singing together at the top of our lungs. The bus ride home can be the best time of the day. I bet the California kids feel lucky because the Beach Boys are from there. Frances is a little conceited since she's from England, like the Beatles. Who's from Connecticut? Nobody who has any hit songs.

Mom made my next appointment with Dr. Hughes, and I am getting worried. His office wanted to schedule it for March 30, but Mom had the brains not to schedule it on my birthday, so it will be the 31st. *Ugh*, I am not looking forward to it.

Thursday, March 26

After choir, I shopped for a birthday present for Margaret. I'm invited to a sleepover at her house tomorrow night. I got her Jean Nate hand lotion because we both love the smell and its French name. I also got her a mug that says "Margaret." They never sell ones that say "Carol-Anne."

Nothing in the *Weston Town Crier* this week about Martin Luther King coming to town but on the *Evening News* tonight,

Walter Cronkite mentioned that Martin Luther King Jr. met with Malcolm X today. I wonder why? Maybe just to talk more about nonviolence and working together.

Saturday, March 28

Yesterday, I took the bus home with Margaret. Mom had taken my overnight bag and present over there during the day. After we ate supper and had birthday cake, Margaret opened her presents. She loved her mug and Jean Nate lotion. Her sister said it stunk but who cares? We both love that lemony smell. We watched TV and gabbed until neither one of us had anything else to say. It was a terrific sleepover even though it wasn't my birthday!

We skipped GFS today and got ready for Easter here at home. Linda and I decorated eggs. After she had gone to bed, Nancy and I hid them for her. That was amusing but I would have preferred being in my room doing nothing.

Sunday, March 29

It's Easter Sunday today so we've got plastic green grass, eggs, chocolate and once again, my favorite: Peeps. We put our Sunday best clothes on, and Mom wore the corsage that Dad had gotten her. No surprise, church lasted way too long. I don't know what the sermon was about because I just sat there, doodled, breathed and took up space until it was time for the choir to sing.

Mom fixed a leg of lamb with potatoes around the pan for dinner. I love the green mint jelly that goes with it. Easter was fine, but it's *my* birthday tomorrow!

Monday, March 30

Hooray! It's my birthday today and it was a good one!

When I stop to think about it, there is something very comforting about not being a brand-new teenager anymore. Somehow, 14 feels much older than 13. In two years, I can get my driver's license.

Mom fixed the dinner I requested, so we had pork chops and rice, applesauce and chocolate cake. I hit the jackpot with the presents. I got clothing from Nana and Aunt Bette, Kakie and Hon. My parents gave me a book of Robert Frost's poems and a silver charm bracelet with a little sailboat charm. My sisters gave me a Beatles album. Mom must have suggested that gift. I got presents from Margaret and Judy, too. Margaret knows I love purple, so she crocheted a lavender scarf for me. She loves making stuff. She told me someday she is going to learn how to use beads to make jewelry.

Judy sent two picture books I can read to Linda, *Where the Wild Things Are* and *The Snowy Day*. She loves all children's books, especially picture books for little kids. She pays special attention to the award-winning ones. I got another silver salad fork from Ahmee and Grandpa. Deposited that right into the camphor chest. They also sent a picture of Ahmee holding the biggest and most beautiful magnolia flower ever. She looks really proud, as if she were holding her own baby.

Ahmee's Pride and Joy!

It's wonderful to be 14, but after the birthday comes the thank-you notes. I'll think about that tomorrow, just like Scarlett O'Hara said in *Gone with the Wind*. Mom and Nana told me there is a new game show they think I'll like. It's called *Jeopardy*.

Tomorrow my pin comes out. I pray I can make it through that doctor's appointment without crying.

Tuesday, March 31

Mom picked me up from school for my doctor's appointment at 1:00. As we neared the drugstore, she asked me if I wanted to stop for an ice cream cone, but I said, "No, I might just throw it right back up." I felt crummy and nervous the entire drive.

When we got into the doctor's waiting room, there was only one other person there, and it was Beth's dad, Harry Reasoner. I recognized him from the *CBS Evening News*. Sometimes he takes Walter Cronkite's place and sometimes he has his own important news show. He had had an accident too. His leg was in a cast. He was buried in a book and never looked up.

I got more and more nervous as I sat and waited to be called, but in the end, it wasn't that bad. They gave me a shot in my finger, something like Novocain. Then Dr. Hughes cut off one side of the pin and pulled the other side through with something that looked like pliers. At least that's what Mom said happened. I didn't look. Thank goodness that's done. My finger is stiff, and it has a little splint that has to stay on for another 10 days, but I can deal with that.

Postscript from Carol-Anne
2020

As I look back, I know that my life was "easy breezy" compared to the lives of black kids and adults. My family and I had plenty of choices and not many worries. We didn't fight for rights or opportunities;

we just took them for granted. Typical, "nothing out of the ordinary" parts of my life were "big deals" for kids and adults whose skin color was different from mine. From my safe, cozy home I watched the struggles of the civil rights movement rush by me.

Sadly, decades later, there continue to be civil rights struggles in our country. I understand now that if I do nothing, it might mean that I am actually making matters worse. I know I have a choice to make. How do I respond? Do I observe or do I act? Do I do anything to encourage and support civil rights efforts? Do I do anything to work towards "liberty and justice for all?"

Well I know that I try. For example, I support agencies that protect and serve children. For example, the Boys and Girls Club and CASA (Court Appointed Special Advocates).

I also support my son Jonathan who is an adult with significant disabilities; he has mental retardation and autism. People with disabilities often face civil rights issues. My husband and I advocate for him and other folks in our community who have disabilities. Our family and friends have encouraged and supported us. This is so important because sometimes advocating can be discouraging, frustrating and exhausting. It can be lonely. When other people "show up" to help "lead the parade" it is a huge gift.

There are lots of opportunities to participate and I participate where I can.

In 1964 when I learned that Martin Luther King Jr. was coming to town, I wanted to hear what he had to say. I was curious about him because his leadership and message was embraced by so many people. I wanted to hear him, really listen and learn more. Maybe I thought that showing up might help in some small way. I know now that I wanted to be there for me, not for others. Today I can see that showing up matters most when it is not just for me, but for other people so that I can support their dreams – perhaps the dreams of freedom that I share with them.

What do you think? Do you participate and support important ideas and projects in your community? What actions do you take? How do you help?

The Telephone Call
April 1964

Thursday, April 2

Quick stop at the card shop after choir today so I could get a birthday present for Judy. No surprise, I am almost running late again. I bought her a box of stationery with puppies on it. She loves dogs, especially her dog Twixie, which she named after the Twix candy bar. This gift will be useful since Judy goes through writing paper faster than anyone I know. When we headed home, Mom told Nancy and me she wanted us to go upstairs and get our homework done before dinner. As we went in, I noticed the dining room table had already been set. I knew something was wrong.

At dinner, Mom and Dad told us Aunt Shirlee and Uncle Tommy were getting divorced. It doesn't seem right. Nothing like this has ever happened in our family before. I don't understand it. I feel bad for Dale and Debbie. Mom and Dad don't have any answers, either. Dad said, "That's just the way it is going to be for them. It's unfortunate but it will be okay."

My parents said my aunt and uncle are going to sell their home in New Jersey. Aunt Shirlee and my cousins are going to live near Ahmee and Grandpa Ray in California. I feel awful.

Friday, April 3

Dance class tonight. Right now, I am sitting under the bouffant cap of my hair dryer, about five minutes from dry. I am "a sight for sore eyes" with this stupid thing on my head. I hope I get to dance with Don. I talked with him a few times at school. Even though he always hangs out with the popular athlete-type guys, he's nice to everyone. Margaret knows Art will dance with her tonight because he has called her a couple of times. More later.

Okay, I am home from dance class, and I'm in bed with my flannel quilt wrapped around me. Dance class was the pits tonight. Just before we were supposed to pick up Margaret, her mom called to say she was throwing up and she couldn't go. Maybe Don was home throwing up, too, because he wasn't there, either. I had to go by myself. Nobody really talked to me even if I tried to talk with them. It's awful being there, and at the same time, not being there. I don't think the dance teachers wanted to be there tonight. They spent the entire time fussing at us kids for no good reason. They didn't even let us do the Twist. I couldn't wait to get home.

I am going to tell Mom and Dad that I am not doing dance class next year. They can save their money.

Wednesday, April 8

There was a little blurb in the *Weston Town Crier* about Dr. King's visit to Westport next month. He's speaking during the Friday evening service at Temple Israel. I bet the people who go there are very excited. It's called a rededication service. I wonder what Dr. King will talk about. I really wish I could hear him in person. I'll talk to Mom about it tomorrow.

Thursday, April 9

My mom and dad don't fight. They "have words," but they don't fight. I am glad about that. I remember a long time ago, the day I met Judy, I was at a new friend's house and I was invited to stay for dinner, but I couldn't because Judy and her family were coming. I was mad at Mom for making me come home, but really, I was kind of relieved.

I went over to Liz's house after GFS. We were in her bedroom listening to records and talking. After a while, I heard voices yelling and getting louder. Liz said her parents "must be having a fight." I had never heard anything like it before. Screaming. Swearing. Stuff being thrown. It was scary, and I could tell Liz was embarrassed. She said, "Let's go down to the barn." I was glad when Mom picked me up.

So, my parents don't fight like that, but they've been "having a lot of words" lately, and I don't know why. Once Mom was crying and I heard her say something about going sideways down the icy hill last winter. Maybe she's still getting over not smoking. Whatever it is, she ought to just quit thinking about it or go read a book.

I asked Mom about me hearing Dr. King speak when he's at Temple Israel next month. She said, "I don't think you should impose on that congregation. He has been invited to speak there, and we aren't members." I wouldn't be *that big* of an imposition.

Friday, April 10

Happy Birthday, Judy! Sorry your present won't be there 'til Monday. I do feel crummy that Judy's present will be late. What is it about me that keeps me from being able to get stuff to her on time?

I listened to Beatles records today after school at Frances's house. When her dad flies to England he always brings back Beatles stuff. Frances knows everything about the Beatles. Today she told me that last week the Beatles had 12 songs on the "Billboard Hot 100" list. Of all the songs she rattled off, I love "Do You Want to Know a Secret" and "Twist and Shout" best.

We had a quick trip to Dr. Hughes's office today. No more splint – and good thing, because the tape was getting smelly.

Sunday, April 12

Today I spent time working through my math homework and reading. Then I put "pen to paper" on a letter to Judy. Even if I don't finish it right away, at least it's started.

Nana and I watched *Ed Sullivan* tonight, and it was stupid. Just a bunch of circus performers from Russia, including a bear trainer, a juggler, a strong man and horseback riders.

Monday, April 13

I love the Temptations. Whenever I'm in my room, I have my transistor radio on in case Murray the K plays their songs. The Temptations are a Motown group. I love Dionne Warwick, too; her voice is terrific. She's had several hits: "Anyone Who Had a Heart," and a new one, "Walk on By." I've memorized the words and when I'm in my room with the door shut, I hold my hairbrush like a microphone and sing along in front of the mirror. Margaret and I were both singing the other day when "Walk on By" came on. It was crazy! I just wish I had the money to buy 45s so I could hear my favorites whenever I want instead of

I wish I had a record player.

waiting for the deejay to play them.

On a more serious note, I *really* want to hear Dr. King speak next month. It's not fair that Mom thinks I'd be an imposition. After all, doesn't Dr. King preach about getting along with each other? People who are different from each other ought to be together, just like when Miss Simpson had us invite the New York GFS girls here. Ever since the fire at Nancy's school, Mom talked about how nice and helpful the Rabbi is to the kids and teachers. If he is, what would it hurt for me to at least ask?

Nana, Mom, and I watched the Academy Awards tonight. Sidney Poitier won Best Actor for his role in *Lilies of the Field*. He was at the March on Washington last summer.

Thursday, April 16

When we got to school, the power was off. Classrooms and hallways were dark, and the bells weren't working. We had homeroom and then got dismissed to second period. No one was counted tardy because nobody was quite sure what time it was. During class time the teachers mostly just talked. Then right before lunchtime, the lights came on and everything was back to normal, except the poor kids who bought hot lunch had to eat it cold. Margaret and I had our usual peanut butter and jelly sandwiches. We felt a little smug. When I got home, Mom told me a squirrel got into the power lines and got fried. When Margaret and I talked on the telephone later, we guessed we had a better day than the squirrel. Of course, Margaret had to say something about the squirrel being nuts.

Friday, April 17

All the kids at school are talking about the World's Fair. It begins next week in Flushing Meadows, New York. I like the theme of the fair: "Peace through Understanding." Sometimes I wonder if there will ever be peace – for everyone, everywhere in the world. A bunch of the kids were talking about how their families will get hotel rooms and stay two or three days. I really wish we could go, but usually my parents don't go in for that kind of thing. Plus, it is supposed to be very expensive.

Summer is just around the corner. The GFS girls are already talking about Holiday House. It is fun just thinking about a return trip. I talked to Mom about it last weekend, and she just said, "We'll see." Usually that means "no." Why wouldn't she let me go this year? I could split the cost with them again. Nancy won't want to go so there's no expense there.

I got a letter from Judy today. Her parents are renting a beach cottage in Rhode Island, and I am invited to come along! They're going for a week. I told Mom and she said to ask which week. I must think of something really fun when Judy visits here, and I don't mean going to Chinatown for Chinese food. She really wasn't too thrilled about that dinner out.

Tuesday, April 21

I have a ton of homework so I can't write much. Nancy was bragging because she doesn't have any today and she did really well on a math test. She always does well in math and never has as much homework as me. Sometimes she really bugs me.

Speaking of Nancy, she got in trouble today with Mom. It must have been *big trouble* because she had to go to her room and put all her books outside the door so she couldn't read while she was being punished. That must have been real torture for her.

Do all big sisters love it when little sisters get in trouble with their parents?

BREAKING NEWS
King IS COMING to Town

Wednesday, April 22

Dr. King made the *Weston Town Crier* today and again, I can't stop thinking about him being just the next town over, so close, and even closer than Bridgeport. Temple Israel is *so lucky* that they will get to hear him speak. Why didn't our minister or Miss Simpson think of this? I talked to Mom about my somehow going but she just shook her head and pooh-poohed the idea like I shouldn't even think about it anymore. I'm disgusted with her being so indifferent. For Pete's sake, he's the 1964 *Time* "Man of the Year" and the youngest person ever to be nominated for the Nobel Peace Prize. She thinks I'm just a kid and shouldn't bother the folks at Temple Israel. Maybe so. Maybe no. Dr. King's visit to the synagogue might not be a big deal to her, but it is to me and I am going to figure out a way to do something about it. It can't hurt to just ask, can it?

Friday, April 24

I talked with Mom today about summer plans with Judy. Since Judy's family wants to take me on their family vacation, I really want her time with us to be special, too. Mom said we might be able to make a trip into New York City, stay overnight with Aunt Bette and then go to the World's Fair. Judy would love that. So, would I. I asked Mom if I could mention it to Judy in my next letter and she said, "Yes." So, I'm off to finish the letter I started two weeks ago, if I can find it.

Saturday, April 25

I've done lots of writing today. I finished an eight-page letter to Judy. I told her that Dr. King is speaking at Temple Israel, and I invited her to come with us to the New York World's Fair. I suggested we make a list of the pavilions we want to see. First on my list? The Pepsi Pavilion, because it has a Walt Disney production called "It's a Small World." It's supposed to be terrific, but the lines are very long. Maybe the lines will be shorter by July.

Still no answer from Mom and Dad about my going to Holiday House again. What's taking them so long?

Sunday, April 26

Yesterday there was something going on at church and they needed babysitters. Janice and I spent six hours in the church nursery entertaining little kids. We sang, read, and played *Duck, Duck, Goose* until we couldn't stand it any longer. We each earned $10.00, and I mean we earned that $10.00. Every cent of it. The kids were okay for about the first two and a half hours, but after that it was a real chore.

Mom and Dad were hardly around this weekend and took a couple of long drives without us girls. Something serious must be going on. I hope they aren't getting a divorce.

Monday, April 27

I can't believe what I did today. I called Temple Israel!

When I got home from school, Mom was on her way out because Linda had a doctor's appointment. Nana needed cigarettes so she went with Mom. I was at home with Nancy and she was practicing her violin. So, with the coast clear, I went looking for – not the *Time* magazine – but the telephone book. I took it upstairs to Mom and Dad's study, a little room just off their bedroom with a desk and a telephone. I closed the doors to the hall and bedroom and looked up the telephone number for Temple Israel. I had already decided I was going to call to ask if I could hear Dr. King speak, even though Mom didn't think I should.

Before I made the call, I took a piece of scratch paper and made a script of what I'd say. Usually I try to avoid making outlines, but this piece of paper was a lifesaver. Then I took a deep breath and dialed the number. I was so nervous, my fingers shook. The dialing was worse than singing my solo on Mother's Day. Finally, the phone rang, and a woman's voice said, "Good afternoon, Temple Israel. How can I help you?" I began to read from my script:

Calling the Rabbi.

Hello, my name is Carol-Anne Hughes. I am 14 years old and I live in Weston. I am calling because I read in the Weston Town Crier *that Dr. Martin Luther King Jr. is going to speak at Temple Israel next month. I am very interested in all of Dr. King's work to encourage non-violence and peace. It may be an imposition, but I am wondering if I might be able to come?*

I think I surprised the lady because at first, she asked me questions. She said, "What did you say your name was?" and "How old are you?" If she told me her name, I didn't get it because I was so anxious, I was shaking. She told me she was the Temple secretary and not the person I really needed to talk to. Then she asked, "Can I get your telephone number so Rabbi Rubenstein can return your call?"

My mind went blank. When I looked down at the number on the telephone dial, I saw that it was our old Pennsylvania number. Just before she would think I was crazy, I remembered our Connecticut telephone number and said it. She repeated it back to me and told me she would speak to the Rabbi. After I hung up, I sat at the desk for the longest time. I'd really done it. I wonder if it will work.

Tuesday, April 28

I told Margaret today about the telephone call. She was amazed. She didn't know I was interested in hearing Dr. King speak. I forgot to tell her, I guess. She thought it was a little sneaky to call without asking. But I already knew what the answer would be, so why ask? I wrote to Judy about it, too. I can't wait to hear what she has to say. I'm pretty sure Judy will think I was very daring like Nancy Drew.

I didn't get a call back from Temple Israel.

Thursday, April 30

When I got home from choir today, Nana handed me a piece of paper that said "Rabbi Rubenstein, Temple Israel. Please call back after school on Wednesday, May 6." I squealed. Mom immediately asked, "What's this all about?" That's when I told her about my call. She shook her head and said, "You should have asked," but she didn't yell. I was relieved. After a while, she volunteered to tell Dad and that's good news. I'll find out at supper tonight.

P.S. Dad was surprised that I wanted to hear Dr. King speak but he wasn't upset. He was much more matter of fact than Mom. Now it seems like next Wednesday will never come.

Postscript from Carol-Anne
2020

In 1964, I was a quiet, shy kid. When I discovered that I wanted to hear Dr. King speak I'm sure I thought it really wasn't possible because he was so famous. I am not sure why but when I talked with my parents, they did not encourage me. But still I got my plan.

Against my parents' wishes, I called Temple Israel to ask if I could hear Dr. King speak. I was so nervous. Calling seemed risky because I didn't know anyone who attended services there and because I was afraid the answer would be "No."

When I was 13 and 14, I wasn't very confident about myself. Since I had attended four different elementary schools in four different states (New Jersey, California, Pennsylvania, and Connecticut), I didn't feel totally at ease at school because I didn't have lots of friends. I really wanted to do well in school, but I rarely got the very best grade on any assignment. I struggled some in math, but I did okay in my other subjects. I was very nervous about calling because I was unsure of myself and making the call seemed like a huge step outside my own "comfort zone."

What if Rabbi Rubenstein thought I was "too young to know what I think?" What if he thought I was a child and that "children should be seen and not heard?"

The Meeting
May 1964

Friday, May 1

The funniest thing happened. After dinner, Nancy was supposed to dish out chocolate pudding. I was going upstairs to get ready for dance class and I heard Nancy say, "Daaaad, there's a snake in the kitchen!" So, I stopped and listened. Dad was ignoring her. Nancy repeated, "Dad, there's a snake in the kitchen and I'm not going in until it's out!" Linda chimed in, "I want my chocolate pudding."

I went back to the dining room in time to see Mom give Dad the evil eye, so he got up and got a broom. We all followed. Yes, there was a little snake in the kitchen. Dad swept it right out the door, but it took a little doing and a little dancing on Dad's part. We all screamed, watching Dad and the snake. When it was over, I said, "Dad's dancing is better than the boys in dance class."

I'm home from dance class now and finally, in the very last class, I had a nice time. I danced with Don twice. Margaret danced with Art, and she told me she was happy because even when she wasn't dancing with him, she could tell he was watching her. On the way home, she said to me, "You should marry Don. He is taller than you and his last initial is the same as yours. Crazy! Margaret, I don't think I'll get married, and if I do, it won't be until after I've had a chance to do what I want with my life.

Sunday, May 3

Every once in a while, something happens that's big news. It happened today and it wasn't about my cousins' family. It was about mine. When Linda was down for her afternoon nap, our parents called Nancy and me into the living room. When they told us both to sit down, I knew something was up.

First, they talked about how unhappy Dad was at work and how he is so tired of the long commute. They said they want more family time. Dad is always gone by 7:00 in the morning. He doesn't get home until 7:00 at night, so dinner is always late. He barely gets to see Linda. Then they talked about how miserable Mom was driving on the icy hills in the winter. I remember her screaming when the car slid down the hill sideways and crying when she drove me to have my finger looked at. Then, after a certain amount of song and dance, they said, "We are moving to California."

I sat there stunned, trying to understand. Moving to California?

They began to babble about the chance to live near Ahmee and Grandpa and Aunt Shirlee, Dale and Debbie. Nana will come with us. They talked about the fine weather, the beaches, sailing with Uncle Van, and on and on. I didn't really listen. Dad is quitting his job, and we are moving to California. When they were finished, I went to my room, shut the door and cried. After a while, Mom came in. She told me to call Margaret from her study. I told Margaret what was going on here and she cried with me. All I could think of was that stupid song Mom drags out every time we move. *"Make new friends, keep the old. One is silver, the other gold."* I don't care about that dumb kid song. I don't want to move and lose Margaret, the best friend I've ever had.

Dad's leaving on Mother's Day. He'll find a job in San Diego. Mom will stay here, pack up, sell the house and then she, Nana, Linda, Nancy and I will drive to California sometime in the summer. No Holiday House this year. This is a miserable plan.

Monday, May 4

I am so sad, deep-down sad, about moving again. Mom tells me I'll be fine. Does that mean I'm not miserable inside? No, I'm not fine. It's going to be really hard to lose Margaret. Her friendship is like Judy's – constant, true and so much fun. They both know me, know who I really am. In a way, Judy and Margaret are my cheerleaders, and I try to be theirs. Margaret's my home-game cheerleader and Judy is away. I'm not so worried about my friendship with Judy. That's mostly been through our letters and those can keep on, even after we move. We started our friendship one silly evening with our dads who are still best buddies after so many years of not seeing each other. Last summer, we loved telling people we are "third generation" friends. I don't know when I'll see her again after this summer, but I'll just always send her stationery for birthday and Christmas presents.

Margaret is another story. We see each other almost every day. We've been through so much: classes and lunchtimes, overnights, dance class, and those horrible jingle bell skirts, our "Maybe So" and "BZ Boys" lists. It's too much to forget.

Next year, I'll be replaced by some nameless, faceless ninth-grade girl who needs a friend and, lucky for her, Margaret will be perfect. I will have to start all over again and hope that I can find someone like Margaret in San Diego. So much energy and work. I wonder if Margaret will be pen pals with me.

Tuesday, May 5

I have another report due for history class, and I don't feel like doing it. As I was working hard to avoid the issue, I remembered a report I did last year in social studies class on "Gothic Architecture." I felt pretty good about it when I turned it in but when I got my graded report back, the teacher noted that I misspelled the word "architecture" every time. I spelled it "architeXture." Good thing Mr. Bowman didn't know about it or he wouldn't have made my spelling champion plaque.

Tomorrow is Wednesday and I am skipping Girl Scouts. I have completed all the requirements and I'm just waiting for the First Class Scout ceremony at the end of the month. My scouting days are over. Tomorrow is also the day I call Rabbi Rubenstein. I am nervous but so happy that he will talk to me. Maybe there's a chance I can go. If it doesn't work out, at least I will have tried.

Wednesday, May 6

I am so wound up and excited. I don't think I have been this excited – ever. I came home from school today and got ready to make my call to Rabbi Rubenstein. I made a shorter script this time:

Hello, my name is Carol-Anne Hughes. I am 14 years old and I live in Weston. I am returning Rabbi Rubenstein's call. I was told to call back after school, Wednesday.

I called from Mom and Dad's study. The same woman's voice answered the telephone, "Good afternoon, Temple Israel. How can I help you?" I read right from my script and the lady said, "Just a minute, please. The Rabbi is expecting your call."

Before too long, a man said, "Hello, Carol-Anne. It's so nice to finally talk with you." Rabbi Rubenstein seemed to take me very seriously. He asked how I found out about this event. That was an easy one: the *Weston Town Crier*. Then he said, "Why do you want to hear Dr. King speak?"

I shared my feelings about the civil rights movement; I told him that I think life is easier for me than it is for Negro kids. I wish our country could be – I think it *should* be – a fair country for all Americans, not just white people. Kids should go to school together regardless of race and that the Jim Crow laws were wrong. I told him I was at my church, singing in our children's choir, when the four choir girls from Birmingham were killed.

I told him about our GFS club and how the New York City GFS girls had come out for a slumber party, how they were all Negro girls, and how we had a wonderful weekend together. I said I always read *Time* magazine and not just the "People" section but the "Civil Rights" part, too. I said our ministers and several people from church went to the March on Washington and I'd watched Dr. King speak then and other times when he was on TV. I said he's a minister who wants "liberty and justice for all" people and that's why I wanted to hear him speak in person.

When I finished talking, there was a pause at the other end of the line. Meanwhile, I was in shock because I had rattled off so much. I figured I'd probably said too much. I was beginning to feel awful. Then the Rabbi said, "Well, you seem quite informed about the civil rights movement. I can tell you're really interested. You know, this is a very special event for Temple Israel. The Temple will be crowded with our regular congregation members."

There was another pause and my heart dropped. At least I'd tried.

"Even so," he said, "I'd like to invite you and your mother or father to our service that evening. You should be there."

I was stunned but I did manage to say, "Thank you so much, Rabbi."

As Rabbi Rubenstein gave me the details of the service, I wrote them down. He told me to let the Temple secretary know which one of my parents would come with me. Then he said, "If I could arrange it, would you like to meet Dr. King and talk with him briefly before the service?"

I wasn't sure I had heard right, so I said, "Pardon? I'm sorry I don't think I heard you."

Rabbi Rubenstein said again, "Would you like to meet and talk with Dr. King?" I couldn't believe my ears, but Rabbi Rubenstein made it clear that if I was interested, he would find out if it was possible for me to talk to Dr. King. Of course, I said, "Yes!"

As our conversation finished up, I was trembling. All I had to do was find out if Mom could take me to the Temple at 9 p.m. on Friday, May 22, and all the Rabbi had to do was check with Dr. King's "people." Rabbi Rubenstein said he'd call me back when he knows something. Ouch! I must pinch myself... this is really happening to me!

Thursday, May 7

I'm so excited about being able to attend the service at Temple Israel: it takes my mind off moving to California. At school, Margaret and I talked about the move. We've come up with several solutions to help Mom deal with driving in bad weather, but we can't think of anything that would shorten Dad's commute. Since Margaret moved recently, she knows what I am in for. She thinks it's horrible that my parents want to leave Connecticut. I agree and I've even thought maybe Dad won't be able to get a job out there. That wouldn't be good for our family, but it would be good for me.

Maybe Margaret could move with us.

Friday, May 8

Today Mom told me that she and Dad talked things over and tomorrow she is taking me to Saks Fifth Avenue in White Plains to shop for a dress to wear to Temple Israel. She said she hasn't got time to make something new. Aunt Kakie is meeting us there to shop for something that will look nice with my yellow spring coat and pillbox hat.

A store-bought dress. Oh boy! Some dreams do come true!

Saturday, May 9

No GFS for me today. We got up early and drove to White Plains. Nana came along. It was a whirlwind experience because my great aunt, grandmother, and mother, plus the saleslady, were all there to find a dress for me. Nana and Mom worked through the racks very slowly and systematically. Not Kakie. She flipped through the hangers so fast, I was surprised she even saw the dresses. She'd say, "No, not this one. Here, try this one," holding her choices out for someone else to take. Eventually, they identified about 20 dresses to try on, and I went to the dressing room with the saleslady. It was like clockwork. Put the dress on. Exit the dressing room and go to the mirror. Show the ladies and listen to their input. Go back to the dressing room, change into the next dress and start the process all over. I knew we weren't leaving until I had a dress. Dress number 18 proved to be just right. It is a powder blue shift with a crew neck and contrasting yellow piping. It's perfect even though Mom didn't make it.

After a nice lunch with Aunt Kakie, we drove back to

Connecticut. Dad insisted on a fashion show. New dress, with yellow spring coat and pill box hat. I feel so lucky. Nancy was jealous that I got a store-bought dress and that I get to hear Dr. King speak. Well, I am jealous of all the attention she gets when she plays her violin. It's my turn this time.

Sunday, May 10

It's Mother's Day. After church and our little celebration for Mom and Nana, Mom took Dad to the train station. He has a late flight to California tonight. Everybody was sad when he left because nobody is sure what will happen. His last day at work was Friday and who knows when his next day at work will be? Nana is certain everything will work out. Still, so much of what's going on here on Merry Lane seems unsure. I could tell Mom had been crying when she got back from the station. We ate cereal for dinner, had a bowl of ice cream, and watched *Ed Sullivan*.

It's my cousin Debbie's birthday. They're getting ready to move, too.

Tuesday, May 12

This evening, my window was open, and I heard some sounds outside. When I looked out, I saw a huge buck with antlers moseying up the hill toward Route 57. He must have heard something because suddenly he started to run. His hooves clicked on the street and then he leaped high over the fence that runs parallel to the street. That was a beautiful sight, one I probably won't see in San Diego.

Dad called Mom tonight. He's staying with Ahmee and Grandpa and will start looking for a job tomorrow. Mom's news was that our refrigerator is not moving to California because the handle broke. We are using masking tape to keep the door closed. It is a pain in the neck. We'll probably go through about 100 rolls of masking tape before we head west.

Wednesday, May 13

When I got home from Girl Scouts today, Nana had a message for me from Rabbi Rubenstein. *It's great news!* Dr. King said he would like to meet me! *Unbelievable!* The Rabbi said Mom and I should come very early, at 8 p.m., and sit in the car until Dr. King's motorcade arrives. When it does, I should join the welcoming committee, and then the Rabbi will introduce me.

At Girl Scouts today, we were finalizing the plans for the Awards Ceremony. It is going to be nice but with all that's going on in my life, it's not as big a deal as it once was.

Saturday, May 16

Margaret stayed over last night. It was our usual silliness. Records were on, and we used our hairbrushes as we sang into the mirror over the mantle. It was great until Mom yelled, "Turn it down!" We danced the Mashed Potato, the Twist and the Monkey. We talked about Don and Art. She thinks Art is her boyfriend, but I don't know about Don. He is kind of shy. Never mind. I'm moving. We got talking about my move again and we both got teary. The school year is about over and when it is, she's going to Georgia for the summer. She'll get back to Connecticut after we have left for California. It makes me sick to think about.

I could tell that Mom was feeling blue this morning. She is still eating lots of cheese, so she doesn't start smoking again. She misses Dad. She has lots to do to get ready for the move. After lunch we did something, she said she's always wanted to do. She's a big fan of Dave Brubeck, and he lives in Wilton. He's a famous pianist and travels around with his jazz group. Someone at GFS told her he was back in town. So, we packed snacks and drove over toward his place. As we got near, Mom slowed way down and, with our heads out the windows, we listened for music. He was playing! So, we continued a little way past his mailbox and parked and had our own private concert. He was probably just practicing but even that sounded good. He played "Take 5." Mom was so happy.

Monday, May 18

While we were at school, the real estate agent came by. The "For Sale" sign goes up Thursday. The idea of leaving here and moving to San Diego makes me sick but I do miss Dad. The "For Sale" sign will force me to think of this Merry Lane house as part of our past. I've been through this before and for the first time, since I am older, I am thinking about it in a different way. Home can be a house, but it doesn't have to be. Home can be the family you love, shortcomings and all. Home doesn't have to just be your house and family. I'm at home in my letters to Judy and when we are together, even if we are fighting. I'm at home with Margaret, wherever we are and whatever we are doing. But I wonder if Margaret and I do write letters, will our friendship be the same? Maybe so. Probably no.

Tuesday, May 19

The World's Fair trip is on for sure, and I am happy about that except that it seems like a bribe. Mom's feeling guilty and came up with this as a payoff to me for moving and helping her pack all the boxes. In exchange, I get a one-day visit to the World's Fair, a last overnight at Aunt Bette's, and Judy gets to come, too. She thinks this is a fair deal. Not even close, Mom.

I got a letter from Judy today. Mostly it's our combined World's Fair "Must See" list that includes Great Moments with Mr. Lincoln, Progressland, Michelangelo's Pieta, the Swiss

Sky ride and It's a Small World. Judy's in for a few surprises when she comes. She doesn't know it yet, but she'll be packing boxes too. I'm definitely not telling her about our broken refrigerator door handle. That will drive her nuts faster than it has the rest of us.

Thursday, May 21

Choir was fine. One more day to the *big* day!

Friday, May 22

Today I am going to meet Dr. Martin Luther King Jr. I am going to hear him speak in person! At school, I kept thinking about tonight. When I got home, Mom had my newly cleaned yellow spring coat hanging up in the front hall closet. My new shift is hanging from my bedroom door. I'll change after we've eaten dinner so if I make a mess, it doesn't matter. More later.

It's after 11:30. Mom and I got home about 10:45. Nana and Nancy waited up so we could tell them all about the Rededication Service at Temple Israel. They wanted to hear about my meeting with Dr. King. We are all still so amazed it really happened. But before I forget, I want to write about everything that came before the drive to Westport.

We ate dinner early, just macaroni and cheese since Dad's not here. Mom and I watched the clock because we didn't want to be in a last-minute rush; we planned to leave the house at 7:30. As the time to leave got closer, Nancy sulked because she wanted desperately to go, too. I felt a little sorry for her. Nana hugged me on the way out and whispered, "Carolee, remember everything so you can tell me all about it." I smiled and nodded.

It was still quite light when we turned into the synagogue's driveway. Temple Israel is set back off the main road. There were only a few other cars there already when Mom pulled into the parking lot. We settled in to wait. I was pretty edgy. Mom kept talking quietly but I couldn't think about what she was saying. I knew she was trying to keep me calm but it wasn't working. Soon we knew we weren't the only ones waiting for the guest of honor. A man dressed in a light gray suit came out of the synagogue. Then a couple of others followed. Mom said, "There's the Rabbi." She pointed to a man a little shorter than Dad, with dark-rimmed glasses. He seemed to be in charge. The men clustered together and watched the driveway. Mom and I figured they were the welcoming party.

I'll finish up my story about meeting Dr. King tomorrow. I'm so tired.

Saturday, May 23

It took me forever to get to sleep last night. I was tired but was still wound up. Murray the K eventually lulled me to sleep. I'll finish writing about last night before I go down for breakfast.

Soon after the Temple Israel welcoming committee came out to the parking lot, a limousine and two other black cars pulled into the entrance and slowly came down the driveway. Doors opened and several well-dressed Negro men climbed out. Among them was Dr. Martin Luther King Jr.

THE RENEWAL OF OUR HERITAGE...

I caught my breath and said, "Mom, there he is." She reached over, squeezed my hand and replied, "Well, then, you'd better go. Don't forget to smile." I opened the car door, straightened my yellow spring coat and crossed the parking lot. My eyes were on Dr. King. He looked so familiar to me, just like his pictures in the news. The man with

The Rabbi, Dr. Martin Luther King Jr., and President of the Congregation.

the dark-rimmed glasses saw me coming and drew the guest of honor's attention to me. As I neared the group of men, he reached out his hand to shake mine and said, "Hello, Carol-Anne? I am Rabbi Rubenstein. I'm glad to meet you. Let me introduce you to Dr. King."

Martin Luther King Jr. turned his dark eyes on me, and we shook hands. Then with a warm smile and a deep voice, he said, "Hello, Carol-Anne. I am pleased to meet you. Rabbi Rubenstein shared a little bit about your interest in the civil rights movement, but I wish you'd tell me yourself."

And so, I started in to tell him about the events I witnessed on TV. Children arrested. Protestors attacked by police dogs and hit with billy clubs. I told him how sad I'd been when the four choir girls were killed. I also told him about some of our church sermons and the Girls' Friendly Society.

Dr. King asked, "What church do you attend?" and I told

him, "St. Matthew's Episcopal Church in Wilton." I knew they didn't have all day, so I quickly told them about the slumber party and weekend together with the New York City GFSers and how when the New York City girls came for the visit, I learned they were just girls like me. I said, "We should all have the same choices and chances and go to school together all across the country."

Dr. King smiled and kept his gaze on me all the time I was talking. The smiling Rabbi stood next to him and nodded as I spoke. He had already heard my story. I ended by saying, "I think that all the work you do will make our country a better place for all people. Thank you." Dr. King replied, "I appreciate that. I'm happy to hear about the gathering with your new friends from New York City. That's so wonderful. And now we have tonight." He turned to include Rabbi Rubenstein. "Isn't it wonderful, Carol-Anne? Isn't it a gift that our Jewish friends have invited us – Christians, you and me – into their synagogue for this special service? This is how it is supposed to be, all God's children, brothers and sisters, together. I believe God wants us all to be His heart and hands as we live our lives every day." I smiled and nodded. The other people around us ended their conversations and were waiting.

"Perhaps now we'd better go in and get ready for the service. It was a pleasure meeting you, Carol-Anne." Then he turned to walk inside the Temple. Rabbi Rubenstein beckoned for me to follow along with the welcoming committee and the other people with Dr. King. Mom had come near while I was talking. I could tell she was proud of me. Other people were arriving and were craning their necks to see Dr. King. At the synagogue door, an usher came forward, and after a word with the Rabbi, he led Mom and me to good center seats. The inside of the Temple reminded me of our church. The seats faced front. There was a raised lectern for the speaker and a table for the holy books.

We didn't see Rabbi Rubenstein and Dr. King for another half hour. The room filled up and some people were standing in the back. Finally, the service started. The Rabbi came in, followed by Dr. King and several others. The program talked about people rededicating themselves to justice for all. Dr. King's speech sounded so familiar. He said, "the time is now for all God's children – all Americans – to come together, work together to create real American change: liberty, justice and freedom for all." When he made a point, I could see members of the Temple Israel congregation nodding in agreement. The people who had come in the cars with him also nodded; some people said, "Amen!" When Dr. King was finished, there was a hush over the audience, and I think if we weren't in a sacred space, people would have clapped a long time. After it was over, it took forever to get out of those good seats and to the car and home. I didn't see Dr. King again. Maybe there will be something about his visit in the paper next week.

Sunday, May 24

Yesterday at GFS, Miss Simpson wanted to hear about the Rededication Service. She asked me to share my experience with the other GFSers, so I told them all about meeting Dr. Martin Luther King Jr. It was fun to be center stage. Dad called today to talk with me, and it wasn't just a "quick hi." He wanted to hear about Friday night, and I could tell he was interested. He realized I wasn't too young to know what I thought about meeting Dr. Martin Luther King Jr.

He had news about his job hunt. It's over already, and he and Mom are thrilled. Now we just have to sell the house. Before long, we will head west and be together again. Dad suggested we put a sign on the station wagon that says, "California or Bust." Not such a great idea, Dad. Mom's doubly excited because someone came to see the house yesterday and they're scheduled to come back for a second look. *Ugh.* We'll have to straighten up all over again.

Face the facts, Carol-Anne. We're moving – and soon.

Monday, May 25

Memorial Day today. Food but not much family fun. No flag because there's no one tall enough to put it up. Nana and I watched the Kentucky Derby today, but Dad wasn't here to say, "Place your bets," so we didn't.

I looked at the Rededication Service program again today. The program is great because it has the whole service written out. Except for the parts that were in Hebrew, I followed along with everything. Some of the prayers sounded like prayers we have at St. Matthews. We prayed for justice, the oppressed, the fatherless and the widows, and strangers. We always pray for those people at my church, too. One prayer said, "Hate evil and love the good and establish justice in your gates." That's what Mr. Greene has been preaching forever. The choir sang "May the words of my mouth and the meditations of my heart be acceptable to Thee, my Rock and my Redeemer." I've heard that hundreds of times. In the program, Rabbi Rubenstein wrote, "Compassion brings us very near to our neighbor who suffers. Justice urges us to seek equality for the Negro; compassion helps us feel for him and moves us to acts of sacrifice when justice is thwarted." That message sounds so familiar.

Dr. King was right about that evening being "all God's children together."

I wonder what my diary would look like if Rabbi Rubenstein hadn't returned my call. Instead of having a wonderful memory of meeting Dr. Martin Luther King Jr., it would be a bunch of whining from a 14-year-old. I can be good at whining. Mom suggested I write a short thank-you note to the Rabbi. Here's a first draft:

> Dear Rabbi Rubenstein,
> Thank you so much for inviting me to Temple Israel last Friday night. I really wanted to hear Dr. King speak but meeting him was even better. If it hadn't been for you, this wouldn't have been a dream come true.
> The Rededication Service and Dr. King's sermon reminded me about what I have been thinking about at my church and especially in my Girls' Friendly Society club. Many of the words I heard were so familiar to me – justice, compassion, equality, and personal success. I've learned lessons from Dr. King and from you. I believe these lessons should be passed on, which reminds me of a song I learned at camp last year, "This Little Light of Mine." It says we should all let our lights shine. Dr. King's light shines. I hope my light will shine for someone just as yours and his did for me.
> Sincerely yours,
> Carol-Anne Hughes

Wednesday, May 27

After supper tonight, Mom drove Nana, Nancy, Linda and me up to the Congregational Church for the Girl Scout year-end ceremony. Mrs. Conley gave me and Margaret, Deirdre and Ellen our First Class Girl Scout pins. I worked hard and was happy to earn the award. I came home, tucked the pin into my jewelry box and felt a little sad. I've known for a long time that my Girl Scout days would end and now they have.

Saturday, May 30

Nancy and I got a surprise today when we went to GFS. The meeting was a going-away party for the two of us. Everybody had gone in together to get a cake, card and present. We got a new book, *Happiness is a Warm Puppy*. I'm not crazy about comics but everybody loves *Peanuts*. Snoopy is Nancy's favorite but I like Charlie Brown. The girls at GFS think moving is an adventure. Well, maybe so, but I'd rather skip it. I know I'll feel lost and alone in a new place. I've moved enough to know that eventually I'll settle into life in San Diego, but it will take time. I'll have to plod through bumpy situations and a fair amount of loneliness until I am really comfortable and happy in a new city.

Postscript from Carol-Anne
2020

Years later, I realized that Rabbi Rubenstein was a great role model for me – in fact, a hero. I had just a few interactions with him, but he taught me important life lessons I can't forget. I think of the Rabbi as an American citizen who was also a patriot.

He was a teacher. Teachers work to support, encourage and hopefully, inspire their students. It seems to me that the Rabbi wanted to teach, lead and help people understand the importance of joining in, participating at this critical time in our history. The Rabbi's actions showed others what they could do to support and contribute to the civil rights movement. Weeks after the service in Westport, Connecticut Rabbi Rubenstein took part in a demonstration in St. Augustine, Florida. He was arrested and spent two days in jail.

When I first spoke with Rabbi Rubenstein, he "showed up." He was there to take my call. He listened carefully to me, asked questions, and understood my story, my point of view. In an instant, I felt encouraged and supported. And lucky for me because he helped my dream – my "Connecticut Journey" come true. I am forever grateful.

At the same time, Dr. King was willing to talk with me that evening in the parking lot at Temple Israel. He too, listened and quickly, his words "connected" with me. Although our skin colors were different, he spoke of what we had in common and our shared hopes for the future.

Showing up and listening. Taking action. Hope. These ideas are lessons I learned at that time and lessons I took into my classroom when I was an elementary school teacher and a professor who pre-

pared new teachers for the elementary classroom.

What is patriotism? Do you think the Rabbi was a patriot? Why or why not?

June 1964

Saturday, June 6

We're packing up, so there are boxes, newspapers, tape and junk galore all over the place. When I ask Mom where something is, she just says, "In a box." We're never going to be able to find anything again until – forever.

Margaret's house seemed so peaceful by comparison when I stayed there last night, even with her brother and all the extra sisters. We rode her bus home, watched TV, ate dinner, and talked and talked. Before we went to bed, Margaret said, "I want to show you something." She went over to her dresser and gently lifted a cut crystal bell from the dresser top. As she showed me, I oohed and aahed. It was a beautiful bell and sounded so sweet. She told me her mom gave it to her for Christmas.

"Mom said it would help me forget about the jingle bells at the bottom of that stupid Christmas skirt," Margaret explained. "She said I needed something to help me get over that miserable night." We laughed together. That memory is something we will always share, awful though it was. Then

Margaret pulled a small gift-wrapped box from her top dresser drawer. "Open it. It's for you," she said. I unwrapped the box and found a cut crystal bell, exactly like hers. I rang it and smiled. Margaret continued, "I am calling it a friendship bell, our friendship bell. Take it with you to California. Put it on your dresser so that you will remember me back in Connecticut. Even though we were friends here for just one short school year, let's be friends forever." She leaned toward me and gave me a hug.

Sounds super to me, Margaret. You are just like Judy. The best.

Postscript from Carol-Anne
2020

Our family move to California brought new challenges and opportunities. It was hard to move so far away from my friends Judy and Margaret. But good friendships last and we are friends still – even fifty years later.

We still need people who believe in "liberty and justice for all" and people who will take action so that dream can come true. Just as President Kennedy said, "One person can make a difference." Even one young child or one teenager can lead the way towards change for the good. Ruby Bridges, a six-year-old black girl, integrated a public school in New Orleans, Louisiana; she made a huge contribution to the struggle for equal rights and access for all people. Since the publication of her diary, Anne Frank, although not an American, has been an inspiration to so many people because of the strength of her human spirit. Another example is Janie Forsyth, a twelve-year-old white girl from Anniston, Alabama. In May 1961 black and white Freedom Riders traveled south to register black citizens to vote. An angry mob forced the bus to stop and then set the bus on fire outside Janie's family's market. Frightened passengers escaped from their bus. Janie rushed to give them water. I think back and ask myself: would I act like Janie?

My point of view? Our country still needs work. We need more people like Ruby Bridges, Anne Frank and Janie Forsyth. Who are the others? Maybe it is you!

It took the civil rights movement to wake me up to the fact that there were many people who were forced to live totally different lives because their skin color was darker than mine or their religion was different than mine. I know that every one of us – kids and adults – can listen and learn, show up, help by taking action when needed and be a glimmer of hope to someone in need. It's a choice that each of us makes.

What choices will you make as you journey forward?

Author Biography

Carol-Anne Hossler is a retired educator who taught in public schools in Oxnard, California, and Chicago, Illinois, for fourteen years. She was the lead teacher at a private elementary school in Elgin, Illinois. After a move to Bloomington, Indiana, she became an elementary principal, earned a doctorate in educational leadership, and then taught at Indiana University. She worked with students in the elementary education program and taught classes that provided prospective teachers opportunities to consider and discuss the civil rights movement.

Carol-Anne is married and has three sons; one son has significant life challenges due to mental retardation and autism. In her spare time, she enjoys family – especially her granddaughter, friends, gardening, and advocacy. She supports and works for adults with disabilities. As a court-appointed special advocate with CASA, she works with children in need of services.

Bibliography

Bass, Patrik H. *Like a Mighty Stream: The March on Washington, August 28, 1963.* New York: Running Book Press, 2002.

Bennett, Lerone. *What Manner of Man: A Biography of Martin Luther King Jr.* Chicago: Johnson Publishing Company, 1964.

Evers-Williams, Myrlie. *Watch Me Fly: What I learned on the way to becoming the woman I was meant to be.* New York: Little, Brown and Company, 1999.

Farnham, Thomas. *Weston: The Forging of a Connecticut Town.* West Keenebunk, MA: Phoenix Publishing, 1980.

Frank, Anne. *Anne Frank: The Diary of a Young Girl.* New York: Bantam Books, 1993.

Hunt, George P. (1963, December 6). Caroline said, "I only cried twice." Life, Vol. 55, No 23, p.3.

Kasher, Steven. *The Civil Rights Movement: A Photographic History*, 1954 – 68. New York: Abbeville Press, 1996.

King, Correta S. *My Life with Martin Luther King Jr.* New York: Holt, Rhinehart and Winston, 1969.

Lee, Harper. *To Kill a Mockingbird.* New York: Harper Collins, 1960.

McWhorter, Diane. *A Dream of Freedom: The Civil Rights Movement from 1954 to 1968.* NY: Scholastic, Inc., 2004.

Meltzer, Milton. *There Comes a Time: The Struggle for Civil Rights.* New York: Random House, 2001.

Nichols. (1964, May 23). King Speaks at Temple Israel: King Defends 'Potent Weapon.' The Bridgeport Post, p.4.

Stoughton, Cecil. (1964). White House Photographs. John F. Kennedy Presidential Library and Museum, Boston.

Time. (March, 1963 – June, 1964).

www.ingramcontent.com/pod-product-compliance
Lightning Source LLC
Chambersburg PA
CBHW020406080526
44584CB00014B/1202